The Success Blueprint: Learning and Cultivating Essential Habits

Pille Pat Du

Published by Pille Pat Du, 2024.

THE SUCCESS BLUEPRINT: LEARNING AND CULTIVATING ESSENTIAL HABITS

First edition. April 2, 2024.

Copyright © 2024 Pille Pat Du.

ISBN: 979-8224261161

Written by Pille Pat Du.

Table of Contents

Chapter 1: Introduction

- OVERVIEW OF THE SUCCESS Blueprint

Success is a concept that is both universal and personal. While the definition of success may vary from person to person, there are certain principles and strategies that can be applied by individuals in order to achieve their goals and fulfill their dreams. This is where the concept of a Success Blueprint comes into play.

A Success Blueprint is a plan or strategy that outlines the steps and actions needed to achieve success in a particular area of life. It serves as a roadmap that guides individuals towards their goals and helps them stay focused and motivated along the way. The key elements of a Success Blueprint include setting clear and specific goals, developing a plan of action, staying committed to the process, and making adjustments as needed.

Setting clear and specific goals is the first step in creating a Success Blueprint. This involves defining what success means to you and identifying the specific outcomes you want to achieve. Whether it's starting a successful business, advancing in your career, or improving your health and well-being, knowing what you want to accomplish is essential in creating a roadmap for success. By setting clear and specific goals, you can create a vision for your future and establish a sense of purpose and direction.

Once you have established your goals, the next step in creating a Success Blueprint is to develop a plan of action. This involves breaking down your goals into smaller, manageable tasks and creating a timeline for when each task will be completed. By creating a plan of action, you can ensure that you are taking the necessary steps towards achieving your goals and staying on track. Additionally, having a plan in place can help you prioritize your tasks, manage your time effectively, and overcome obstacles that may arise along the way.

Commitment is another key element of a Success Blueprint. Success does not happen overnight, and achieving your goals requires dedication, perseverance, and a willingness to put in the effort needed to succeed. By staying committed to the process and staying focused on your goals, you can overcome challenges, stay motivated, and push through setbacks. It's important to remember that success is a journey, not a destination, and staying committed to your goals is essential in achieving the success you desire.

Flexibility is also an important aspect of a Success Blueprint. While it's important to have a plan in place, it's equally important to be open to making adjustments as needed. Life is unpredictable, and obstacles and challenges may arise that require you to change course or adapt your approach. By being flexible and willing to make adjustments to your plan, you can navigate through challenges and setbacks more effectively and continue moving forward towards your goals. By setting clear and specific goals, developing a plan of action, staying committed to the process, and being flexible in your approach, you can create a roadmap for success that guides you towards the life you desire. Success is within reach for those who are willing to put in the effort, stay committed to their goals, and remain focused on their vision for the future. With a Success Blueprint in place, you can turn your dreams into reality and create the life you've always wanted.

- Importance of Cultivating Essential Habits

Cultivating essential habits is crucial for personal and professional growth. Habits are the actions that we repeat regularly and unconsciously, shaping our behaviors and ultimately determining our success in life. Developing positive habits can lead to increased productivity, improved health and well-being, and overall happiness. Conversely, negative habits can hinder our progress and hold us back from reaching our full potential. Therefore, it is important to consciously cultivate essential habits that will support our goals and aspirations.

One of the key benefits of cultivating essential habits is the impact they have on our productivity. By establishing routines and rituals that support our work and goals, we can streamline our workflow and focus our energy on tasks that matter most. For example, incorporating a habit of daily planning and prioritizing tasks can help us stay organized and efficient in our work, leading to greater productivity and success. By cultivating essential habits that promote focus and discipline, we can eliminate distractions and stay on track with our goals, ultimately leading to increased productivity and success.

Another important aspect of cultivating essential habits is the impact they have on our health and well-being. Habits such as regular exercise, healthy eating, and adequate sleep play a crucial role in maintaining our physical and mental health. By cultivating these essential habits, we can improve our overall well-being, increase our energy levels, and reduce our risk of chronic diseases. Additionally, habits such as mindfulness and stress management can help us cope with the challenges of everyday life, leading to greater resilience and mental well-being. By cultivating essential habits that support our health and well-being, we can optimize our performance and thrive in all areas of our lives.

In addition to productivity and health, cultivating essential habits is also crucial for personal growth and development. Habits such as continuous learning, goal setting, and self-reflection can help us expand our knowledge, skills, and perspectives. By cultivating these essential habits, we can become lifelong learners, constantly evolving and improving ourselves. Additionally, habits such as gratitude and kindness can help us cultivate positive relationships and contribute to our overall happiness and fulfillment. By consciously cultivating essential habits that promote personal growth and development, we can unlock our full potential and achieve our goals and aspirations. By establishing routines and rituals that support our goals and aspirations, we can increase our productivity, improve our health and well-being, and achieve personal growth and development. Whether it is through habits that promote productivity, health, or personal growth, it is important to consciously cultivate essential habits that will support our success and happiness in life. By taking the time to identify and cultivate these essential habits, we can create a solid foundation for achieving our goals and living a fulfilling life.

Chapter 2: Understanding the Power of Habits

- DEFINITION OF HABITS

Habits are a fundamental aspect of human behavior that play a crucial role in shaping our daily lives. They are defined as the routine actions or behaviors that are performed regularly and automatically, often without conscious thought. Habits can be both positive and negative, and they can have a significant impact on our overall well-being and success.

One of the key characteristics of habits is their automatic nature. Once a behavior becomes a habit, it is performed almost unconsciously, requiring little or no effort or thought. This automaticity is what distinguishes habits from other types of behavior, such as intentional actions or decisions. For example, brushing your teeth before bed may be a habit that you do without thinking, while deciding to go for a run in the morning is a conscious choice that requires effort and motivation.

Another defining feature of habits is their regularity. Habits are behaviors that are repeated consistently over time, often on a daily or weekly basis. This repetition reinforces the behavior and makes it more ingrained in our routines. For example, if you make a habit of going to the gym every morning before work, the more you do it, the more likely it is to become a natural part of your daily routine.

Habits can be formed in a variety of ways, but they are typically developed through a process of reinforcement and conditioning. When we engage in a behavior that is rewarding or pleasurable, our brain releases dopamine, a neurotransmitter that reinforces the behavior and encourages us to repeat it.

Over time, this reinforcement strengthens the neural pathways associated with the behavior, making it more automatic and difficult to change.

On the flip side, habits can also be formed through negative reinforcement. For example, if we consistently turn to unhealthy coping mechanisms when we are stressed or anxious, those behaviors can become habits that are difficult to break. This is why it is important to be mindful of the habits we cultivate and to actively work towards forming positive habits that promote our well-being and success.

Breaking bad habits and forming new ones can be challenging, but it is possible with persistence and dedication. One strategy for breaking bad habits is to identify the triggers that lead to the behavior and to develop alternative coping mechanisms. For example, if you tend to stress eat when you are feeling anxious, you could try going for a walk or practicing deep breathing exercises instead. By replacing the habit with a healthier behavior, you can gradually rewire your brain and break the cycle of negative reinforcement. They can be both positive and negative, and they play a crucial role in influencing our actions and decisions. By understanding the nature of habits and how they are formed, we can empower ourselves to make positive changes and cultivate habits that support our well-being and success. With mindfulness and dedication, we can break bad habits and form new ones that enhance our lives and help us reach our goals.

- How Habits Influence Our Daily Lives

Habits play a significant role in shaping our daily lives, influencing our behavior, decisions, and overall well-being. Defined as routine behaviors that are performed automatically, habits have a profound impact on our actions and thought processes. Whether positive or negative, habits can contribute to the formation of our character and the trajectory of our lives. In this essay, we will explore the ways in which habits influence our daily lives, the mechanisms behind habit formation, and strategies for cultivating healthy habits.

One of the key ways in which habits influence our daily lives is through their ability to streamline our actions and conserve mental energy. Habits allow us to execute routine tasks with minimal effort and conscious thought, freeing up cognitive resources for more complex activities. For example, brushing our teeth or driving to work may require little mental effort because these actions have become ingrained habits. By automating certain behaviors, habits enable us to navigate our daily lives more efficiently and effectively.

Furthermore, habits can serve as powerful drivers of behavior, shaping our choices and actions in both positive and negative ways. For instance, if we have developed a habit of exercising regularly, we are more likely to prioritize physical activity and maintain a healthy lifestyle. Conversely, if we have a habit of procrastinating, we may struggle to meet deadlines and achieve our goals. Understanding the influence of habits on our behavior can empower us to consciously cultivate positive habits and break free from detrimental ones.

The formation of habits is a complex process that involves a combination of psychological, neurological, and environmental factors. Habits typically develop through a three-step process known as the habit loop, which consists of a cue, a routine, and a reward. The cue serves as a trigger for the habit, signaling the brain to initiate the routine behavior. The routine is the habitual behavior itself, while the reward is the positive reinforcement that reinforces the habit loop. By understanding the components of the habit loop, we can identify the cues that trigger our habits, alter the routines to create healthier behaviors, and seek alternative rewards to reinforce positive habits.

To cultivate healthy habits and break free from detrimental ones, it is essential to adopt strategies that promote behavior change and habit formation. One effective approach is to set specific, measurable, achievable, relevant, and time-bound (SMART) goals that align with our values and priorities. By setting clear objectives and creating a plan for achieving them, we can increase our motivation and commitment to changing our habits. Additionally, implementing environmental cues and reminders can help reinforce new habits and reduce the reliance on willpower alone. Surrounding ourselves with supportive individuals and engaging in activities that align with our desired habits can also bolster our efforts to create lasting change. By understanding the mechanisms behind habit formation and implementing strategies for cultivating healthy habits, we can empower ourselves to lead more fulfilling and balanced lives. Through conscious effort and consistent practice, we can harness the power of habits to create positive change and achieve our goals. Ultimately, by embracing the role of habits in our daily lives, we can unlock our potential for growth, resilience, and personal transformation.

- Breaking Bad Habits and Creating New Ones

Breaking bad habits and creating new ones is a common challenge that many people face in their everyday lives. Habits are ingrained behaviors that we perform automatically, often without even realizing it. Whether it's biting your nails, procrastinating, or overeating, breaking these habits can be difficult but not impossible. By understanding the psychology behind habits and implementing strategies to change them, individuals can successfully break bad habits and create new ones.

The first step in breaking bad habits is to identify the root cause of the behavior. Habits are often formed as a way to cope with stress, boredom, or other emotions. By recognizing the triggers that lead to the habit, individuals can begin to understand why they engage in the behavior and work towards finding healthier alternatives. For example, someone who overeats when they are stressed may benefit from finding other stress-relief techniques such as exercise or meditation. By addressing the underlying cause of the habit, individuals can begin to break free from its grasp.

Once the root cause of the habit has been identified, individuals can begin to implement strategies to break the habit and create new ones. One effective strategy is to replace the bad habit with a healthier behavior. For example, someone who smokes when they are stressed could try chewing gum or going for a walk instead. By replacing the old habit with a new, healthier one, individuals can begin to rewire their brains and create new, positive behaviors.

Another strategy for breaking bad habits is to set clear, achievable goals. It's important to set realistic goals that can be easily measured and tracked. For example, if someone wants to stop procrastinating, they could set a goal of completing a certain task each day without putting it off. By setting small, achievable goals, individuals can build momentum and create a sense of accomplishment that will motivate them to continue breaking the habit.

In addition to setting goals, individuals can also benefit from seeking support from friends, family, or a therapist. Breaking bad habits can be a challenging process, and having a support system in place can make it easier. Whether it's talking to a friend about your progress or seeking professional help, having someone to hold you accountable can make a big difference in breaking bad habits and creating new ones.

It's also important to practice self-compassion and patience when trying to break bad habits. Changing ingrained behaviors takes time and effort, and it's important to be kind to yourself along the way. If you slip up or have a setback, don't be too hard on yourself. Instead, acknowledge the mistake, learn from it, and move forward. By practicing self-compassion and patience, individuals can create a positive mindset that will help them successfully break bad habits and create new ones. By identifying the root cause of the habit, implementing strategies to change it, setting achievable goals, seeking support, and practicing self-compassion, individuals can successfully break free from old habits and create new, positive behaviors. It's important to remember that changing habits takes time and effort, but with persistence and determination, anyone can make positive changes in their lives.

Chapter 3: Building a Strong Work Ethic

- IMPORTANCE OF WORK Ethic in Achieving Success

Work ethic is a crucial element in achieving success in any endeavor. It is the underlying principle that drives individuals toward their goals and helps them maintain focus and determination in the face of challenges. Work ethic can be defined as the set of values and attitudes that a person holds towards their work and the effort they put into achieving their goals. It encompasses qualities such as diligence, perseverance, dedication, and a strong sense of responsibility.

One of the key reasons work ethic is so important in achieving success is that it is directly linked to productivity and performance. Individuals with a strong work ethic are more likely to put in the time and effort required to excel in their chosen field. They are committed to doing their best work and constantly strive to improve their skills and knowledge. This dedication and determination translate into higher levels of productivity, efficiency, and effectiveness, which ultimately lead to success.

Another reason why work ethic is essential for success is that it sets individuals apart from their peers. In today's competitive and fast-paced world, having a strong work ethic can give individuals a distinct advantage over others. Employers, clients, and colleagues are more likely to trust and respect those who demonstrate a strong work ethic. They are seen as reliable, responsible, and trustworthy, which can open doors to new opportunities and advancements in one's career.

Furthermore, work ethic plays a critical role in helping individuals overcome obstacles and setbacks on their path to success. The road to achieving one's goals is rarely smooth, and setbacks, failures, and challenges are inevitable. However, individuals with a strong work ethic are better equipped to persevere through difficult times. They have the resilience and determination to bounce back from setbacks, learn from their mistakes, and keep moving forward towards their goals.

In addition to productivity, differentiation, and resilience, work ethic also fosters a sense of personal satisfaction and fulfillment. When individuals put in the effort and dedication required to achieve their goals, they experience a sense of accomplishment and pride in their work. This intrinsic motivation drives them to continue striving for success and fuels their passion for what they do. As a result, they are more likely to find fulfillment and happiness in their careers and personal lives.

It is important to note that work ethic is not just about working hard for the sake of working hard. It is also about working smart, setting clear goals, and prioritizing tasks effectively. Individuals with a strong work ethic are able to manage their time and resources efficiently, focus on high-priority activities, and make strategic decisions that contribute to their success. By combining hard work with strategic thinking, individuals can maximize their productivity and achieve their goals more effectively. It is the driving force that propels individuals towards their goals, helps them overcome obstacles, and fosters personal satisfaction and fulfillment. By cultivating a strong work ethic and embodying qualities such as diligence, perseverance, and dedication, individuals can maximize their productivity, set themselves apart from their peers, and navigate the challenges of achieving success. Ultimately, work ethic is not just a trait that leads to success; it is a mindset and a set of values that shape one's approach to work and life.

- Developing Discipline and Consistency

Developing discipline and consistency is an essential skill that can greatly enhance one's personal and professional life. It involves the ability to control one's actions, thoughts, and habits in a consistent and focused manner. By cultivating discipline and consistency, individuals can achieve their goals, improve their productivity, and maintain a sense of balance and well-being in their lives.

One of the key factors in developing discipline and consistency is setting clear and achievable goals. It is important to have a clear understanding of what you want to achieve and to establish a plan for reaching your goals. By breaking down your goals into smaller, manageable tasks, you can create a roadmap to success and stay on track with your progress. Setting realistic deadlines and milestones can also help you stay motivated and focused on your objectives.

Another important aspect of developing discipline and consistency is creating a routine and sticking to it. Establishing a daily routine can help you build good habits and instill a sense of structure in your life. By consistently following a routine, you can train your mind and body to operate more efficiently and effectively, leading to improved productivity and overall well-being. Additionally, having a routine can help you avoid distractions and stay focused on your priorities.

Practicing self-discipline is another key factor in developing discipline and consistency. Self-discipline involves the ability to control your impulses, emotions, and behaviors in order to stay on track with your goals and responsibilities. By practicing self-discipline, you can develop a strong sense of willpower and resilience, which can help you overcome obstacles and challenges that may arise along your journey. Setting boundaries for yourself and learning to say no to distractions can also help you stay focused and committed to your goals.

Consistency is another important aspect of developing discipline. Consistency involves the ability to remain steadfast and committed to your goals and routines over time. By consistently practicing good habits and behaviors, you can create positive momentum in your life and achieve lasting success. Consistency can also help you build trust and credibility with others, as they will see you as reliable and dependable.

In order to develop discipline and consistency, it is important to cultivate a growth mindset. A growth mindset involves the belief that your abilities and intelligence can be developed through effort and hard work. By adopting a growth mindset, you can embrace challenges and setbacks as opportunities for growth and learning, rather than seeing them as obstacles to your progress. This shift in perspective can help you stay motivated and resilient in the face of adversity, and can empower you to achieve your goals with confidence and determination.

Building discipline and consistency is a lifelong journey that requires dedication, persistence, and self-awareness. By setting clear goals, creating a routine, practicing self-discipline, and cultivating a growth mindset, you can develop the skills and habits needed to achieve success in all areas of your life.

Remember that developing discipline and consistency is a gradual process, and it is important to be patient and kind to yourself as you work towards your goals. With time and effort, you can cultivate the discipline and consistency needed to reach your full potential and lead a fulfilling and meaningful life.

- Overcoming Procrastination

Procrastination is a common issue that many people struggle with in their daily lives. It is the act of putting off tasks or responsibilities until a later time, often leading to feelings of guilt, stress, and unproductivity. While procrastination can be a habit that is difficult to break, there are strategies and techniques that can help individuals overcome this behavior and become more efficient and successful in their endeavors.

One of the first steps in overcoming procrastination is to understand why it happens in the first place. Procrastination is often a result of fear, perfectionism, lack of motivation, or poor time management skills. By identifying the root cause of your procrastination, you can start to address the underlying issues and develop strategies to combat them. For example, if you find that you are procrastinating because you are afraid of failure, you can work on building your self-confidence and resilience to face challenges head-on.

Another important aspect of overcoming procrastination is setting specific and achievable goals. Many people procrastinate because they feel overwhelmed by the sheer amount of work that needs to be done. By breaking down tasks into smaller, more manageable chunks, you can make the process feel less daunting and more achievable. Setting deadlines for yourself can also help to keep you accountable and motivated to complete tasks in a timely manner.

It is also essential to create a work environment that is conducive to productivity. This may involve minimizing distractions, such as turning off notifications on your phone or finding a quiet place to work. By creating a space that is dedicated to focusing on your tasks, you can eliminate potential excuses for procrastination and increase your chances of successfully completing them.

In addition, creating a schedule or routine can help you stay on track and avoid procrastination. By setting aside specific times each day to work on tasks, you can establish a sense of structure and discipline that can help you overcome the urge to procrastinate. It is important to prioritize tasks based on their importance and deadlines, so you can allocate your time and energy efficiently.

Another helpful strategy for overcoming procrastination is to utilize tools and techniques that can enhance your productivity. This may include utilizing time management apps, creating to-do lists, or using the Pomodoro technique, which involves working in short bursts with breaks in between. By finding tools and techniques that work for you, you can streamline your workflow and minimize the likelihood of procrastination.

It is also important to practice self-care and maintain a healthy work-life balance to prevent burnout and reduce the likelihood of procrastination. Getting enough sleep, eating well, exercising regularly, and taking breaks when needed are all essential factors in maintaining your overall well-being and productivity. By taking care of yourself, you can improve your focus, motivation, and energy levels, making it easier to overcome procrastination and stay on track with your tasks.

Ultimately, overcoming procrastination requires self-awareness, discipline, and perseverance. By identifying the root causes of your procrastination, setting specific goals, creating a conducive work environment, establishing a schedule, utilizing tools and techniques, practicing self-care, and maintaining a healthy work-life balance, you can successfully overcome procrastination and become a more efficient and productive individual. With determination and effort, you can break the cycle of procrastination and achieve your goals with confidence and success.

Chapter 4: Cultivating a Positive Mindset

- THE IMPACT OF MINDSET on Success

The concept of mindset has gained significant attention in recent years as research has shown a strong correlation between mindset and success. Mindset refers to the way individuals view their abilities and intelligence, and it can be broadly categorized into two main types: a fixed mindset and a growth mindset. A fixed mindset is characterized by the belief that abilities and intelligence are static and predetermined, while a growth mindset is characterized by the belief that abilities and intelligence can be developed through effort and perseverance.

Individuals with a growth mindset are more likely to embrace challenges, persist in the face of setbacks, and see failure as an opportunity for growth. They are also more likely to seek out feedback and use it constructively to improve their skills. On the other hand, individuals with a fixed mindset are more likely to avoid challenges, give up easily when faced with setbacks, and see failure as a reflection of their abilities. This can lead to a self-limiting mindset that hinders personal and professional growth.

The impact of mindset on success can be seen in various aspects of life, including academic achievement, career success, and overall well-being. In academic settings, students with a growth mindset tend to perform better in school, as they are more likely to put in the effort required to succeed and view challenges as opportunities for learning. They are also more likely to exhibit resilience in the face of academic setbacks and seek out resources to help them improve.

Similarly, individuals with a growth mindset tend to excel in their careers as well. They are more likely to take on challenging projects, seek out opportunities for growth and development, and adapt to changes in the workplace. They are also more likely to build strong relationships with colleagues and leaders, as they are open to feedback and willing to learn from others.

Overall well-being is also impacted by mindset, as individuals with a growth mindset tend to have a more positive outlook on life and are better equipped to handle stress and adversity. They are more likely to engage in healthy habits, seek out support when needed, and maintain a sense of optimism even in difficult times. Developing a growth mindset can lead to increased resilience, motivation, and overall well-being, while a fixed mindset can hinder personal and professional growth. By recognizing the impact of mindset on success and actively working to cultivate a growth mindset, individuals can unlock their full potential and achieve their goals.

- Strategies for Maintaining a Positive Attitude

Maintaining a positive attitude is essential for success in both personal and professional endeavors. A positive attitude not only influences our own mood and mindset but also affects those around us. It can help us overcome challenges, achieve our goals, and foster positive relationships with others. However, maintaining a positive attitude is not always easy, especially in the face of adversity or setbacks. In this discussion, we will explore various strategies for cultivating and sustaining a positive attitude in different aspects of our lives.

One key strategy for maintaining a positive attitude is to practice gratitude. Taking the time to reflect on and appreciate the things we have in our lives can help shift our focus from what we lack to what we are blessed with. This can help us cultivate a sense of abundance and contentment, even in difficult times. Gratitude can be practiced in various ways, such as keeping a gratitude journal, expressing thanks to others, or simply taking a moment to savor the little things in life. By making gratitude a regular practice, we can train our minds to look for the positive aspects of our lives and maintain a more optimistic outlook.

Another important strategy for maintaining a positive attitude is to surround ourselves with positive influences. The people we interact with, the media we consume, and the environments we spend time in can all have a significant impact on our mindset. By seeking out and engaging with positive and uplifting people, content, and spaces, we can create a more conducive environment for maintaining a positive attitude. This may involve setting boundaries with negative influences, seeking out supportive relationships, and actively seeking out sources of inspiration and motivation. By curating our social and environmental surroundings in a way that fosters positivity, we can strengthen our own optimistic outlook.

In addition to practicing gratitude and surrounding ourselves with positive influences, it is important to cultivate self-care habits that support our mental and emotional well-being. Taking care of ourselves physically, emotionally, and mentally can help us build resilience, manage stress, and maintain a positive attitude even during challenging times. This can include engaging in regular physical activity, getting enough sleep, eating a balanced diet, practicing relaxation techniques, and seeking support from others when needed. By prioritizing self-care and making it a consistent part of our routine, we can better cope with life's ups and downs and maintain a more positive outlook.

Furthermore, setting and pursuing meaningful goals can also help us maintain a positive attitude. Having a sense of purpose and direction can provide motivation, focus, and a sense of fulfillment, which can contribute to a more positive mindset. By setting specific, attainable goals that align with our values and aspirations, we can create a sense of progress and achievement that can boost our confidence and optimism. Additionally, breaking down larger goals into smaller, manageable steps can help us stay motivated and maintain a positive attitude throughout the journey. Celebrating our successes along the way and learning from our setbacks can also help us stay positive and resilient in the face of challenges. By practicing gratitude, surrounding ourselves with positive influences, prioritizing self-care, and setting meaningful goals, we can cultivate and sustain a positive mindset even in the face of adversity. These strategies can help us build resilience, optimism, and a sense of well-being that can enhance our quality of life and contribute to our overall success. By incorporating these strategies into our daily lives, we can create a more positive and fulfilling experience for ourselves and those around us.

- Dealing with Failure and Setbacks

Failure and setbacks are an inevitable part of life, both personally and professionally. It is unrealistic to expect that we will never encounter obstacles or experience disappointments along our journey. However, it is how we choose to respond to these challenges that ultimately defines our character and determines our future success. In this discussion, we will explore strategies for dealing with failure and setbacks in a constructive and positive manner.

One of the most important things to remember when facing failure is to maintain a growth mindset. Instead of viewing setbacks as permanent roadblocks, it is crucial to see them as opportunities for learning and growth. By reframing our perspective in this way, we can extract valuable lessons from our experiences and use them to inform our future actions. This approach not only helps us to bounce back from failure more resiliently, but also fosters a sense of continuous improvement and development.

Another key aspect of dealing with failure is to practice self-compassion and forgiveness. It is natural to feel disappointed, frustrated, or even ashamed when things do not go as planned. However, it is important not to dwell on these negative emotions and instead to show ourselves the same kindness and understanding that we would offer to a friend in a similar situation. By allowing ourselves to make mistakes and acknowledging that they do not define our worth or abilities, we can move forward with a sense of grace and humility.

Additionally, seeking support from others can be instrumental in navigating through failure and setbacks. Whether it be friends, family members, mentors, or colleagues, having a strong support system can provide valuable perspective, encouragement, and guidance in times of struggle. By opening up about our challenges and vulnerabilities, we allow others to offer their insights and assistance, ultimately helping us to feel less isolated and more empowered to tackle our obstacles head-on.

In the face of failure, it is also important to remember to set realistic goals and expectations for ourselves. Oftentimes, setbacks arise when we set overly ambitious or unrealistic targets, leading to feelings of disappointment or inadequacy when we fall short. By establishing clear and achievable goals, we can create a more manageable path to success and reduce the likelihood of experiencing major setbacks along the way. Furthermore, breaking down larger goals into smaller, more attainable milestones can help us to track our progress and stay motivated throughout the process.

Lastly, it is essential to practice resilience and perseverance when dealing with failure. While setbacks can be discouraging and challenging, it is crucial to push through adversity and continue to move forward towards our goals. By maintaining a positive attitude, staying focused on our long-term objectives, and adapting our strategies as needed, we can overcome even the most daunting obstacles and emerge stronger and more determined on the other side. Remember, failure is not the end of the road, but rather a stepping stone towards greater success and personal growth.

Chapter 5: Setting SMART Goals

- UNDERSTANDING THE SMART Criteria

The SMART criteria is a widely used framework for setting and achieving goals in various aspects of life, including business, education, and personal development. The acronym stands for Specific, Measurable, Achievable, Relevant, and Time-bound. By adhering to these criteria, individuals can increase the likelihood of successfully reaching their objectives.

Starting with the first element of the SMART criteria, being specific is essential for effectively setting goals. A specific goal is clearly defined, leaving no room for ambiguity or misinterpretation. For example, instead of setting a vague goal to "improve my presentation skills," a specific goal would be "enroll in a public speaking course to enhance my ability to engage and persuade audiences. " By being specific, individuals can create a roadmap for achieving their goals and measure progress along the way.

Moving on to the second element, goals should be measurable to track progress and determine success. Measurable goals are quantifiable, allowing individuals to gauge their performance and adjust their strategies if necessary. For instance, instead of setting a goal to "increase sales," a measurable goal would be "achieve a 15% growth in sales revenue by the end of the quarter. " By establishing specific metrics to track progress, individuals can stay motivated and focused on reaching their objectives.

The third element of the SMART criteria is ensuring that goals are achievable. Setting realistic goals that are within reach is crucial for maintaining motivation and avoiding frustration. It is important to consider resources, capabilities, and constraints when setting goals to ensure they are attainable. For example, if an individual's goal is to "run a marathon in three months," but they have never run more than a few miles at a time, it may be more realistic to set a goal of "participate in a 5k race within three months and gradually increase distance to prepare for a marathon."

The fourth element of the SMART criteria is ensuring that goals are relevant to the individual's overall objectives and aspirations. Setting goals that align with personal values, interests, and long-term plans increases motivation and commitment to achieving them. It is important to assess the significance of a goal in relation to one's overall priorities and make adjustments as needed. For example, if an individual is pursuing a career in marketing but sets a goal to learn a new programming language, they may need to reconsider whether this goal is directly relevant to their career aspirations.

The final element of the SMART criteria is making goals time-bound by setting deadlines for achievement. Establishing a timeframe for reaching goals provides a sense of urgency and helps individuals prioritize tasks accordingly. Without a deadline, goals can easily be pushed aside or forgotten, leading to procrastination and lack of progress. By setting specific timelines, individuals can create a sense of accountability and work towards achieving their goals in a timely manner. By ensuring that goals are Specific, Measurable, Achievable, Relevant, and Time-bound, individuals can increase their chances of success and stay focused on their objectives. By adhering to these criteria, individuals can create a roadmap for success and track their progress along the way. Whether setting goals in business, education, or personal development, the SMART criteria provides a valuable framework for achieving desired outcomes.

- Creating Action Plans to Achieve Goals

Setting goals is an essential part of personal and professional development. However, simply setting goals is not enough to ensure success. In order to achieve your goals, it is important to create a clear and actionable plan that outlines the steps you need to take to reach your desired outcome. This is where action plans come in.

An action plan is a detailed outline of the specific steps and tasks you need to complete in order to achieve a particular goal. It helps to break down the goal into smaller, manageable tasks that can be completed over time. By creating an action plan, you can track your progress, stay organized, and ensure that you are on the right track to achieving your goals.

When creating an action plan, it is important to start by clearly defining your goal. This will help you to understand what you are working towards and why it is important to you. Once you have a clear understanding of your goal, you can begin to break it down into smaller, more manageable tasks. This will help to prevent feeling overwhelmed and ensure that you stay focused on your objective.

Next, it is important to establish specific deadlines for each task in your action plan. This will help you to stay on track and ensure that you are making progress towards your goal. It is also helpful to set milestones along the way so that you can celebrate your achievements and stay motivated.

In addition to setting deadlines, it is important to assign responsibilities for each task in your action plan. This will help to ensure that each task is completed in a timely manner and that everyone involved knows their role in achieving the goal. By clearly defining responsibilities, you can avoid confusion and ensure that everyone is on the same page.

Communication is also key when it comes to creating action plans. It is important to keep all stakeholders informed of progress, challenges, and changes to the plan. This will help to ensure that everyone is working towards the same goal and can provide support and feedback when needed.

Lastly, it is important to regularly review and revise your action plan as needed. Goals and circumstances may change over time, so it is important to be flexible and willing to adapt your plan as necessary. By regularly reviewing and revising your action plan, you can ensure that you are on track to achieving your goals and make any necessary adjustments to stay on course. By defining your goals, breaking them down into manageable tasks, setting deadlines, assigning responsibilities, communicating with stakeholders, and regularly reviewing and revising your plan, you can increase your chances of success and achieve your desired outcomes. With careful planning and execution, you can turn your goals into reality and make your dreams a reality.

- Reviewing and Adjusting Goals as Needed

Setting goals is an essential part of personal and professional development. Goals provide direction, motivation, and a sense of purpose. However, goals are not static – they may change over time based on a variety of factors such as changes in circumstances, priorities, or resources. It is important to regularly review and adjust goals as needed to ensure they remain relevant and achievable.

There are several reasons why it is important to review and adjust goals as needed. First and foremost, circumstances change. Whether it is personal circumstances, changes in the external environment, or unforeseen events, it is inevitable that things will not always go as planned. By regularly reviewing and adjusting goals, individuals can ensure that they are still on track and working towards the outcomes they desire.

Additionally, priorities may shift over time. What may have been important to someone at one point in their life may no longer hold the same value. By regularly reassessing goals, individuals can determine if their current objectives align with their changing priorities. This can help individuals stay focused and motivated as they work towards achieving their goals.

Furthermore, resources may also play a role in the need to adjust goals. As circumstances change, so too may the resources available to an individual. Whether it is time, money, or other resources, it is important to be realistic about what can be achieved given the resources at hand. By adjusting goals to align with available resources, individuals can set themselves up for success and avoid potential frustration and disappointment.

In order to effectively review and adjust goals as needed, there are several steps that individuals can take. First, it is important to regularly assess progress towards goals. This may involve tracking specific metrics or milestones to determine if progress is being made. By regularly monitoring progress, individuals can identify any potential obstacles or challenges that may need to be addressed.

Second, individuals should consider what has changed since the goals were initially set. This may involve reflecting on personal circumstances, changes in priorities, or shifts in resources. By understanding what has changed, individuals can better assess whether their current goals are still relevant and achievable.

Third, it is important to stay flexible. Goals should be viewed as dynamic and adaptable, rather than fixed in stone. By remaining open to adjusting goals as needed, individuals can ensure that they are able to respond to changing circumstances and stay on track towards achieving their desired outcomes.

To draw to a close, it may be helpful to seek input from others. Whether it is a mentor, colleague, or friend, getting an outside perspective can provide valuable insight and guidance. By discussing goals with others, individuals may gain a new perspective or identify potential blind spots that need to be addressed. By regularly reassessing goals, individuals can ensure that they remain relevant and achievable in the face of changing circumstances, priorities, and resources. By following the steps outlined above, individuals can effectively review and adjust their goals to stay on track towards achieving their desired outcomes.

Chapter 6: Time Management Techniques

- PRIORITIZING TASKS and Responsibilities

Prioritizing tasks and responsibilities is a vital skill in both personal and professional life. In today's fast-paced world, we are constantly bombarded with numerous obligations and deadlines, making it crucial to have a system in place to effectively manage our time and energy. By prioritizing tasks, we can ensure that we are focusing on the most important and urgent responsibilities, thereby increasing our productivity and achieving our goals more efficiently.

One of the key aspects of prioritizing tasks is understanding the difference between important and urgent tasks. Important tasks are those that align with our long-term goals and objectives, while urgent tasks are those that require immediate attention and have pressing deadlines. When prioritizing tasks, it is important to focus on completing important tasks first, as these will ultimately contribute to our overall success and well-being. However, it is also necessary to address urgent tasks in a timely manner to avoid any negative consequences.

In order to effectively prioritize tasks and responsibilities, it is essential to create a system or method that works best for you. One common approach is the Eisenhower Matrix, which categorizes tasks into four quadrants based on their importance and urgency. Tasks are then prioritized based on these criteria, with important and urgent tasks taking precedence over less critical responsibilities. Another popular method is the Pomodoro Technique, which involves breaking tasks into short intervals of focused work, followed by short breaks to increase productivity and focus.

Additionally, it is important to regularly review and reassess your task list to ensure that you are staying on track and making progress towards your goals. By regularly evaluating your tasks and responsibilities, you can identify any potential obstacles or areas where you may need to adjust your priorities.

This can help you stay organized and focused, ensuring that you are effectively managing your time and energy.

In addition to prioritizing tasks, it is also important to delegate responsibilities when necessary. Delegating tasks can help lighten your workload and free up time to focus on more critical tasks. When delegating tasks, it is important to consider the skills and strengths of your team members and assign tasks accordingly. By effectively delegating responsibilities, you can ensure that tasks are completed efficiently and effectively, while also empowering your team members to take ownership of their work.

To wrap up, it is important to remember that prioritizing tasks and responsibilities is not a one-size-fits-all approach. What works for one person may not work for another, so it is important to experiment with different methods and techniques to find what works best for you. By continuously refining your approach to prioritizing tasks, you can increase your productivity, reduce stress, and ultimately achieve your goals more effectively. Remember, effective task prioritization is a skill that can be developed and honed over time, so don't be afraid to try new strategies and approaches to find what works best for you.

- Using Time Blocking for Maximum Productivity

Time blocking is a productivity technique that involves breaking your day into distinct blocks of time dedicated to specific tasks or activities. By allocating a specific time period for each task, you can better focus on the task at hand and avoid distractions. This method is particularly effective for professionals who have a lot of responsibilities and deadlines to juggle.

One of the key benefits of time blocking is that it helps you prioritize your tasks and manage your time more effectively. By assigning specific time slots to each task, you are able to ensure that important tasks are given the attention they deserve. This can help you avoid procrastination and ensure that you are making steady progress on your projects.

Another advantage of time blocking is that it helps you create a routine and structure for your day. By scheduling your tasks in advance, you can create a roadmap for your day and ensure that you are using your time wisely. This can help you stay organized and focused throughout the day, leading to increased productivity and efficiency.

In addition, time blocking can help you manage distractions and interruptions more effectively. By setting aside specific time blocks for tasks that require focus, you can minimize the impact of interruptions on your productivity. This can help you stay on track and complete your tasks in a timely manner.

Furthermore, time blocking can help you achieve a better work-life balance. By allocating specific time blocks for work and personal activities, you can ensure that you are dedicating enough time to both aspects of your life. This can help you avoid burnout and ensure that you are able to maintain a healthy balance between work and personal life.

To effectively implement time blocking, there are a few key strategies to keep in mind. First, it is important to identify your most important tasks and assign them time blocks accordingly. By prioritizing your tasks, you can ensure that you are focusing on the most important and high-impact activities.

It is also important to be realistic when allocating time blocks for tasks. Make sure to give yourself enough time to complete each task without feeling rushed or overwhelmed. It is better to overestimate the time needed for a task than to underestimate it and end up feeling stressed and behind schedule.

Another key strategy for effective time blocking is to batch similar tasks together. By grouping similar tasks into the same time block, you can take advantage of momentum and minimize the time spent switching between different types of tasks. This can help you optimize your productivity and efficiency throughout the day.

It is also important to be flexible with your time blocking schedule. While it is helpful to have a structured plan for the day, it is also important to be able to adjust your schedule as needed. Unexpected events or interruptions may arise, and it is important to be able to adapt and make changes to your schedule as necessary. By allocating specific time blocks for tasks, you can prioritize your work, manage distractions, and create a structured routine for your day. By following key strategies for effective time blocking, you can optimize your time and achieve better work-life balance.

- Dealing with Time Wasters and Distractions

Time management is a crucial skill in today's fast-paced world, where distractions and time wasters abound. Whether you are a student trying to juggle multiple assignments and deadlines, a working professional striving to meet project timelines, or simply a busy individual trying to balance personal and professional responsibilities, learning how to deal with time wasters and distractions is essential for maximizing productivity and achieving your goals. In this discussion, we will explore strategies and techniques for identifying and minimizing time wasters and distractions, as well as practical tips for improving time management to ensure that you make the most of your precious time.

One of the first steps in dealing with time wasters and distractions is to identify and understand the most common sources of wasted time. Procrastination is a major time waster that affects many individuals, leading to delays in completing tasks and projects. Procrastination often stems from a fear of failure, perfectionism, or a lack of motivation. It is important to recognize the signs of procrastination and address them early on to prevent it from becoming a habit. Another common time waster is poor time management, such as overcommitting to too many tasks or failing to prioritize effectively. Without a clear plan and schedule, it is easy to get overwhelmed and lose focus, leading to wasted time and missed deadlines.

Distractions are another significant factor that can derail your productivity and eat away at your time. In today's digital age, technology has made it easier than ever to get distracted, with constant notifications, emails, social media updates, and other online distractions vying for your attention. It is important to set boundaries and establish rules for using technology to prevent it from interfering with your work or study time. Creating a distraction-free work environment, such as turning off notifications, closing unnecessary tabs or apps, and setting specific time blocks for focused work can help reduce distractions and improve your concentration.

Effective time management requires self-discipline and a strong sense of self-awareness. It is important to have a clear understanding of your priorities, goals, and values so that you can make informed decisions about how to allocate your time. This means saying no to tasks or activities that do not align with your goals or values, and setting boundaries to protect your time and energy. Learning to delegate tasks, ask for help when needed, and prioritize effectively can also help you make the most of your time and avoid getting bogged down by time wasters and distractions.

In addition to proactive strategies for managing time wasters and distractions, it is important to develop habits and routines that promote productivity and focus. This includes establishing a daily routine or schedule that allows for consistent work and rest periods, as well as setting specific goals and deadlines to keep you motivated and on track. Taking regular breaks, practicing mindfulness or meditation, and engaging in physical activity can also help you recharge and maintain focus throughout the day. By incorporating these habits into your daily routine, you can create a conducive environment for productivity and success.

When it comes to dealing with time wasters and distractions, communication and collaboration are key. It is important to communicate your priorities and boundaries to colleagues, friends, and family members so that they can support your efforts to manage your time more effectively. Collaborating with others on tasks or projects can help you leverage their skills and expertise to achieve better results in less time. Building a strong support network of mentors, colleagues, and friends who can provide guidance, feedback, and encouragement can also help you stay motivated and accountable in your efforts to overcome time wasters and distractions. By identifying the most common sources of wasted time, setting clear goals and priorities, establishing boundaries, and developing positive habits and routines, you can minimize distractions and maximize your productivity. Remember that time is a valuable resource that cannot be replaced, so it is important to use it wisely and make the most of every moment. With dedication, perseverance, and a proactive approach to time management, you can overcome time wasters and distractions and achieve your goals with greater efficiency and effectiveness.

Chapter 7: Networking and Relationship Building

- IMPORTANCE OF NETWORKING for Success

Networking plays a crucial role in achieving success in both personal and professional endeavors. By connecting with others, individuals can create valuable relationships that open doors to new opportunities, resources, and support. Networking allows individuals to expand their knowledge, gain new perspectives, and stay informed about industry trends and developments. In today's interconnected world, it has become increasingly important to cultivate and maintain a strong network of contacts to thrive in various fields.

One of the key benefits of networking is the access to new opportunities that it provides. By building relationships with a diverse range of individuals, professionals can learn about job openings, collaborations, partnerships, and other opportunities that may not be advertised through traditional channels. Networking allows individuals to tap into the hidden job market, where many positions are filled through referrals and personal connections. By leveraging their network, individuals can gain access to exclusive opportunities and leverage their connections to advance their careers or achieve their goals.

In addition to access to opportunities, networking also helps individuals build their reputation and credibility in their respective fields. By establishing relationships with professionals who are respected and influential, individuals can enhance their own credibility and credibility. When trusted contacts vouch for an individual's skills, experience, and professionalism, it can help open doors to new opportunities, partnerships, and collaborations. Building a strong network of contacts who are willing to endorse and recommend you can help boost your credibility within your industry and increase your chances of success.

Networking also provides individuals with access to valuable resources and support that can help them navigate challenges and overcome obstacles. By connecting with peers, mentors, and industry experts, professionals can tap into a wealth of knowledge, experience, and expertise. Networking allows individuals to seek advice, guidance, and mentorship from those who have walked a similar path or have overcome similar challenges. By leveraging their network, individuals can access valuable resources, information, and support that can help them make informed decisions, overcome obstacles, and achieve their goals.

Moreover, networking can help individuals stay informed about industry trends, developments, and best practices. By connecting with professionals from different backgrounds, industries, and regions, individuals can gain new perspectives, insights, and ideas that can help them stay ahead of the curve. Networking allows individuals to learn from others, attend industry events, conferences, and workshops, and stay informed about emerging trends, technologies, and opportunities. By staying connected with their network, professionals can gain valuable insights and information that can help them make informed decisions, develop new skills, and adapt to changing market conditions. By building and nurturing relationships with a diverse range of individuals, professionals can access new opportunities, gain credibility, access valuable resources and support, and stay informed about industry trends and developments. Networking allows individuals to expand their knowledge, gain new perspectives, and leverage their contacts to achieve their goals and advance their careers. In an era where success is often determined by who you know, networking plays a crucial role in helping individuals thrive and succeed in their personal and professional endeavors.

- Building Meaningful Relationships

Building meaningful relationships is a vital aspect of human interaction that plays a significant role in our personal and professional lives. These connections can bring about a sense of belonging, support, and fulfillment, contributing to our overall well-being and success. However, cultivating and maintaining meaningful relationships requires time, effort, and communication skills. In this essay, we will delve into the importance of building meaningful relationships, explore strategies for developing strong connections, and highlight the benefits of nurturing these bonds.

One of the key reasons why building meaningful relationships is essential is because humans are social beings by nature. We thrive on connections with others, and these interactions provide us with emotional support, encouragement, and a sense of belonging. Building relationships allows us to share experiences, ideas, and emotions with others, fostering a sense of community and unity. Meaningful relationships can also enhance our overall happiness and well-being, as studies have shown that individuals with strong social connections tend to be healthier and live longer lives.

In a professional context, meaningful relationships are crucial for career growth and success. Building rapport with colleagues, managers, clients, and other industry professionals can open doors to new opportunities, collaborations, and mentorship. A strong network of relationships in the workplace can also help increase job satisfaction, boost morale, and improve overall team dynamics. Furthermore, maintaining positive relationships with clients and customers can lead to increased loyalty, retention, and referrals, which are essential for business growth and success.

To build meaningful relationships, it is important to first establish trust and mutual respect with others. Trust forms the foundation of any relationship and is built through consistency, honesty, and reliability. It is also essential to communicate effectively and actively listen to others, showing empathy and understanding. By being present and engaged in conversations, we demonstrate our interest in the other person and strengthen the bond between us. Additionally, showing appreciation and gratitude for others can go a long way in building meaningful relationships, as it conveys respect and value for the individual.

Another key strategy for building meaningful relationships is to invest time and effort in getting to know others on a deeper level. This means being genuine, authentic, and vulnerable in our interactions, sharing our thoughts, feelings, and experiences with others. By being open and transparent, we can create a sense of intimacy and understanding in our relationships, allowing both parties to connect on a more meaningful level. Building emotional intelligence and empathy can also help us navigate conflicts and challenges in relationships, promoting understanding and collaboration.

The benefits of nurturing meaningful relationships are vast and far-reaching. Studies have shown that individuals with strong social connections have lower levels of stress, anxiety, and depression, as well as improved physical health and longevity. In the professional realm, building meaningful relationships can lead to increased job satisfaction, career advancement, and overall success. Strong relationships also provide a support system during tough times, offering comfort, advice, and encouragement when needed. Ultimately, investing in meaningful relationships can enrich our lives, bring joy and fulfillment, and contribute to our overall well-being and success. By investing time, effort, and communication skills in nurturing these connections, we can cultivate strong bonds that provide support, encouragement, and fulfillment. Trust, effective communication, empathy, and authenticity are key components in establishing and maintaining meaningful relationships. The benefits of building meaningful relationships are numerous, including improved well-being, increased job satisfaction, and enhanced success in various aspects of life. Ultimately, prioritizing and investing in meaningful relationships can lead to a more fulfilling and rewarding existence.

- Leveraging Your Network for Opportunities

As professionals, we all understand the importance of networking in our career development. Building a strong network can lead to numerous opportunities and advancements in our careers. However, many individuals may not fully leverage their network to its full potential. In this discussion, we will explore the benefits of networking and provide practical tips on how to effectively leverage your network for opportunities.

Networking is more than just making connections or collecting business cards at events. It is about building meaningful relationships with individuals who can support and guide you in your career. Your network can consist of colleagues, mentors, industry leaders, alumni, and even friends and family. These connections can offer valuable insights, advice, and opportunities that can help you grow and excel in your field.

One of the key benefits of networking is the access it provides to hidden opportunities. In today's competitive job market, many opportunities are not advertised publicly. Instead, they are often filled through referrals and recommendations from within a network. By maintaining strong relationships with individuals in your network, you increase your chances of hearing about these opportunities and being recommended for them.

Another benefit of networking is the opportunity to gain valuable insights and advice from experienced professionals in your field. By connecting with individuals who have more experience or expertise than you, you can learn from their successes and challenges. These insights can help you navigate your own career path more effectively and avoid common pitfalls.

Networking also provides opportunities for collaboration and partnership. By connecting with individuals who have complementary skills or services, you can explore potential collaborations that can benefit both parties. Collaborating with others can lead to new business opportunities, increased exposure, and expanded reach in your industry.

To effectively leverage your network for opportunities, it is important to be proactive in your networking efforts. Building and maintaining relationships takes time and effort, so it is essential to invest in nurturing your connections. This can include attending networking events, reaching out to individuals for informational interviews, and staying in touch with your network through regular communication.

It is also important to be strategic in your networking approach. Identify individuals in your network who can offer the most value in terms of opportunities, insights, and advice. Focus on building strong relationships with these key contacts and nurturing those connections over time. By prioritizing quality over quantity in your network, you can ensure that your relationships are meaningful and beneficial.

In addition, be sure to give as much as you receive in your networking interactions. Networking is a two-way street, and it is important to offer support, advice, and assistance to your connections as well. By being a valuable and supportive member of your network, you will build goodwill and strengthen your relationships, making it more likely that others will be willing to help you in return.

To terminate, remember that networking is a long-term investment in your career. Building a strong network takes time and effort, but the benefits can be significant. By leveraging your network effectively, you can open doors to new opportunities, gain valuable insights and advice, and expand your reach and influence in your industry. So, take the time to invest in your network, nurture your relationships, and be proactive in seeking out opportunities – your career will thank you for it.

Chapter 8: Developing Effective Communication Skills

- THE ROLE OF COMMUNICATION in Success

Communication plays a crucial role in achieving success in various aspects of life, whether it be in the workplace, relationships, or personal development. Effective communication is a key skill that can help individuals navigate through challenges, build strong connections with others, and achieve their goals. In the professional world, communication is essential for fostering collaboration, problem-solving, and making informed decisions. Without clear and concise communication, misunderstandings can occur, leading to inefficiencies, conflicts, and missed opportunities.

One of the primary functions of communication in success is the ability to convey information effectively. Being able to articulate ideas, thoughts, and objectives in a clear and concise manner is essential for ensuring that others understand your message. Whether it is through written, verbal, or non-verbal communication, the ability to express oneself in a way that is easily understood is crucial for successful interactions. In a professional setting, effective communication is essential for conveying important information, delegating tasks, providing feedback, and building relationships with colleagues and clients.

Furthermore, communication is essential for establishing and maintaining strong relationships. By cultivating open and honest communication, individuals can build trust, empathy, and mutual respect with others, fostering positive connections that can lead to shared success. In both personal and professional relationships, effective communication is key for resolving conflicts, addressing concerns, and maintaining a sense of transparency and collaboration. By actively listening to others, expressing empathy, and communicating openly and honestly, individuals can build strong relationships that support personal growth and achievement.

In addition to facilitating collaboration and relationships, communication is also essential for problem-solving and decision-making. Effective communication enables individuals to gather information, share ideas, and work together to identify solutions to challenges and make informed decisions. By engaging in open and constructive communication, individuals can brainstorm ideas, analyze different perspectives, and reach consensus on the best course of action. In a professional setting, effective communication is crucial for overcoming obstacles, adapting to change, and achieving common goals as a team.

Moreover, communication plays a critical role in enhancing personal development and growth. By actively seeking feedback, sharing experiences, and engaging in meaningful conversations, individuals can gain valuable insights, expand their perspectives, and learn from others. Effective communication allows individuals to reflect on their strengths and weaknesses, set goals for personal growth, and seek support and guidance from others. By cultivating strong communication skills, individuals can foster self-awareness, emotional intelligence, and resilience, which are essential for navigating challenges, learning from experiences, and achieving personal success. By honing effective communication skills, individuals can navigate challenges, build strong relationships, solve problems, and achieve personal growth. Whether it is in the workplace, relationships, or personal development, effective communication is essential for fostering collaboration, building trust, and making informed decisions. By actively listening, expressing empathy, and communicating openly and honestly, individuals can cultivate connections that support their journey towards success. Therefore, it is crucial for individuals to prioritize developing their communication skills in order to achieve their goals and create a positive impact in their personal and professional lives.

- Active Listening and Empathy

Active listening and empathy are two essential skills that are crucial for effective communication, building strong relationships, and fostering understanding and connection with others. Active listening is the practice of fully concentrating on what is being said, understanding the content, and responding thoughtfully. It involves not only hearing the words that are spoken but also paying attention to the speaker's tone, body language, and nonverbal cues. Empathy, on the other hand, is the ability to understand and share the feelings of another person. It involves putting yourself in someone else's shoes, seeing things from their perspective, and showing compassion and understanding for their emotions and experiences.

When it comes to active listening, there are several key components that are essential to master. Firstly, it is important to give the speaker your full attention and avoid distractions such as looking at your phone or thinking about your response while they are talking. By being fully present and attentive, you are showing the speaker that you value what they have to say and that you are genuinely interested in listening to them. Additionally, it is crucial to maintain eye contact, nod your head, and use verbal cues such as "I see" or "I understand" to show that you are engaged and following along with the conversation. By actively participating in the dialogue and demonstrating that you are actively listening, you are creating a supportive and respectful environment that encourages open communication and mutual understanding.

In addition to actively listening, empathy plays a significant role in effective communication and relationship-building. Empathy involves not only understanding another person's emotions but also expressing care and compassion for their feelings. When you empathize with someone, you are able to connect with them on a deeper level, validate their experiences, and create a sense of trust and understanding. By showing empathy, you are demonstrating that you are willing to listen, support, and be there for the other person in a nonjudgmental and compassionate way. This can help build stronger relationships, improve communication, and create a more harmonious and respectful environment in both personal and professional settings.

One of the key benefits of active listening and empathy is that they help to foster positive and healthy relationships with others. When you practice active listening, you are showing that you value and respect the other person's thoughts, feelings, and experiences. This can help to build trust, create a sense of mutual understanding, and strengthen the bond between you and the other person. Additionally, by demonstrating empathy and showing that you care about the other person's emotions, you are creating a supportive and compassionate environment that promotes open communication and mutual respect. This can help to resolve conflicts, prevent misunderstandings, and improve the overall quality of your relationships with others.

Furthermore, active listening and empathy can also have a positive impact on your own personal growth and development. By actively listening to others and empathizing with their experiences, you can broaden your perspective, gain new insights, and learn more about yourself and the world around you. This can help you develop a greater sense of self-awareness, emotional intelligence, and empathy towards others. Additionally, by practicing active listening and empathy, you can improve your communication skills, conflict resolution abilities, and emotional resilience, which can benefit you in both your personal and professional life. Ultimately, by honing your active listening and empathy skills, you can enhance your relationships, deepen your understanding of others, and cultivate a more compassionate and empathetic approach to communication and interaction.

- Assertiveness and Conflict Resolution

Assertiveness and conflict resolution are two important skills that are essential for effectively navigating interpersonal relationships and resolving conflicts in a constructive manner. Assertiveness is the ability to express one's thoughts, feelings, and needs in a clear and direct manner, while also respecting the rights and boundaries of others. It involves standing up for oneself and communicating in a way that is confident, honest, and respectful. Conflict resolution, on the other hand, is the process of addressing and resolving disagreements or disputes between individuals or groups in a fair and peaceful manner.

Assertiveness is a key component of conflict resolution, as it enables individuals to assert their needs and communicate their perspectives effectively during conflicts. When individuals are assertive, they are able to express their concerns and emotions in a non-confrontational manner, which can help to de-escalate conflicts and facilitate productive communication. Assertiveness also allows individuals to set clear boundaries, assert their rights, and negotiate mutually beneficial solutions to conflicts. By being assertive, individuals can assert their needs and expectations, leading to healthy and respectful interactions with others.

Conflict resolution involves a series of steps that individuals can take to address and resolve conflicts in an effective and constructive manner. The first step in conflict resolution is to identify and understand the underlying issues that are contributing to the conflict. By examining the root causes of the conflict, individuals can gain insight into the perspectives, needs, and emotions of all parties involved. This can help to facilitate empathy, understanding, and communication between individuals, leading to a more collaborative and cooperative approach to resolving the conflict.

Once the underlying issues have been identified, individuals can move on to the next step in conflict resolution, which involves exploring and evaluating potential solutions to the conflict. This may involve brainstorming ideas, considering alternative perspectives, and engaging in open and honest dialogue with all parties involved. By working together to generate and evaluate possible solutions, individuals can increase the likelihood of reaching a mutually beneficial resolution to the conflict. Collaboration and cooperation are key components of conflict resolution, as they enable individuals to work together to find creative and sustainable solutions to conflicts.

Another important aspect of conflict resolution is negotiation, which involves the process of reaching a compromise or agreement that is acceptable to all parties involved. Negotiation requires individuals to communicate effectively, listen actively, and be willing to make concessions in order to reach a mutually beneficial outcome. By engaging in negotiation, individuals can find common ground, address differences, and work towards a resolution that is fair and satisfactory to all parties involved. Negotiation skills are essential for effective conflict resolution, as they enable individuals to navigate complex and challenging situations with diplomacy and tact.

In addition to assertiveness, conflict resolution also requires individuals to develop effective communication skills, such as active listening, empathy, and problem-solving. Active listening involves listening attentively to the perspectives and concerns of others, without interrupting or judging them. By actively listening to others, individuals can gain valuable insights into their needs, emotions, and perspectives, which can help to foster understanding and empathy. Empathy is the ability to understand and share the feelings of others, and is essential for building trust, rapport, and connection with others. By demonstrating empathy towards others, individuals can create a supportive and validating environment for communication, which can help to de-escalate conflicts and promote collaboration.

Another important communication skill for conflict resolution is problem-solving, which involves identifying and evaluating potential solutions to the conflict, and working towards a resolution that is acceptable to all parties. Problem-solving requires individuals to think critically, analyze complex situations, and consider the implications of different courses of action. By engaging in problem-solving, individuals can address conflicts in a systematic and logical manner, which can help to reduce misunderstandings, promote clarity, and facilitate cooperation. Problem-solving skills are essential for effective conflict resolution, as they enable individuals to navigate difficult situations with confidence and competence. By developing assertiveness, individuals can assert their needs, express their perspectives, and communicate in a confident and respectful manner. By honing conflict resolution skills, individuals can address conflicts in a constructive and collaborative manner, by identifying underlying issues, exploring potential solutions, and engaging in negotiation, active listening, empathy, and problem-solving. By mastering these skills, individuals can build positive and resilient relationships, promote mutual understanding, and create harmonious and supportive environments for collaboration and growth.

Chapter 9: Continuous Learning and Personal Growth

- EMBRACING LIFELONG Learning

In today's rapidly changing world, the concept of lifelong learning has become increasingly important. As technology advances and new industries emerge, workers are required to adapt and acquire new skills throughout their careers to stay competitive in the job market. Lifelong learning is the process of continuously seeking out new knowledge, skills, and experiences to enhance one's personal and professional development. It goes beyond traditional education and training programs, encompassing a mindset of curiosity, self-improvement, and adaptability.

One of the key benefits of embracing lifelong learning is the ability to stay relevant and marketable in an ever-evolving workforce. The skills and knowledge that were once sufficient for a particular job may become obsolete as technology and industry practices change. By engaging in continuous learning, individuals can stay ahead of the curve and remain competitive in their field. Employers also value employees who demonstrate a commitment to personal development, as it shows initiative, motivation, and a willingness to adapt to new challenges.

Furthermore, lifelong learning fosters personal growth and fulfillment. The pursuit of knowledge and skills outside of one's comfort zone can lead to new opportunities, experiences, and perspectives. It can boost confidence, self-esteem, and personal satisfaction, as individuals see the results of their efforts and the impact of their continuous learning on their lives and careers. Lifelong learning can also improve cognitive function, memory, and problem-solving skills, as engaging in new challenges and experiences keeps the brain sharp and active.

Additionally, lifelong learning enables individuals to adapt to changes and challenges in their personal and professional lives. In today's fast-paced world, the ability to pivot, innovate, and problem-solve is essential for success. By continuously seeking out new knowledge and skills, individuals can build resilience, flexibility, and adaptability, allowing them to navigate transitions and setbacks with confidence and grace. Lifelong learners are better equipped to handle change, uncertainty, and ambiguity, as they have the tools and mindset to learn, grow, and succeed in any situation.

Moreover, embracing lifelong learning can lead to a more fulfilling and meaningful life. Learning is a lifelong journey that never ends, and every new skill, experience, or piece of knowledge acquired adds value and richness to one's life. It enhances creativity, curiosity, and passion, as individuals explore new interests, pursue new challenges, and expand their horizons. Lifelong learners are more open-minded, empathetic, and adaptable, as they are constantly exposed to new ideas, cultures, and ways of thinking. This can lead to personal growth, self-discovery, and a deeper understanding of oneself and the world around them. By embracing a mindset of continuous learning, individuals can stay relevant, marketable, and competitive in the workforce, while also fostering personal growth, fulfillment, and adaptability. Lifelong learning is a journey of self-discovery, growth, and transformation that can lead to a more fulfilling, meaningful, and successful life. It is never too late to start learning and expanding your knowledge and skills, so why not embrace lifelong learning today and see where it takes you.

- Seeking Feedback and Self-Improvement

Seeking feedback and self-improvement are crucial components of personal and professional growth. In any endeavor, whether it be in the workplace, academia, or personal relationships, feedback serves as a valuable tool for identifying areas of strength and weakness, as well as providing insight into how one's actions are perceived by others. By actively seeking feedback and being open to constructive criticism, individuals can gain valuable insights that can help them improve their performance and achieve their goals.

Feedback can come in many forms, including formal evaluations from supervisors or colleagues, informal discussions with peers, or even self-reflection. No matter the source, feedback should be seen as an opportunity for growth and development. Instead of viewing feedback as a personal attack or criticism, it is important to approach it with an open mind and a willingness to learn. By receiving feedback in a constructive and positive manner, individuals can use it as a tool for self-improvement and personal development.

Feedback can be especially beneficial in a professional setting, where performance evaluations and feedback from supervisors can help employees understand where they excel and where they may need to improve. Constructive feedback can provide individuals with the guidance they need to enhance their skills, overcome challenges, and achieve their career goals. By actively seeking feedback from supervisors, colleagues, and mentors, individuals can gain valuable insights that can help them grow professionally and advance in their career.

In addition to seeking feedback from others, self-reflection is also an important tool for self-improvement. By taking the time to reflect on one's actions, decisions, and interactions with others, individuals can gain a deeper understanding of their strengths and weaknesses. Self-reflection can help individuals identify areas where they excel and areas where they may need to improve, allowing them to set goals for personal growth and development.

While seeking feedback and self-improvement are essential for personal and professional growth, it is also important to approach these processes with a growth mindset. A growth mindset is the belief that one's abilities and intelligence can be developed through dedication and hard work. Individuals with a growth mindset are more likely to seek feedback, embrace challenges, and persist in the face of setbacks. By cultivating a growth mindset, individuals can approach feedback and self-improvement with a positive attitude and a willingness to learn and grow. By actively seeking feedback from others, being open to constructive criticism, and engaging in self-reflection, individuals can gain valuable insights that can help them improve their performance, overcome challenges, and achieve their goals. By approaching feedback and self-improvement with a growth mindset, individuals can cultivate a positive attitude towards learning and growth, and ultimately achieve greater success in their personal and professional lives.

- Setting Personal Development Goals

Setting personal development goals is an essential aspect of self-improvement and growth. It allows individuals to identify areas in their lives that need improvement and set actionable steps to achieve desired outcomes. Personal development goals can encompass various aspects of life, including career, relationships, health, and personal growth. By setting specific and measurable goals, individuals can track their progress and stay motivated to work towards self-improvement.

One of the key benefits of setting personal development goals is the ability to focus on specific areas of improvement. Without clear goals, individuals may feel overwhelmed and unsure of where to start when it comes to self-improvement. By setting goals that are specific and measurable, individuals can break down larger objectives into manageable tasks and track their progress over time. This sense of clarity and direction can help individuals stay motivated and focused on achieving their goals.

Another benefit of setting personal development goals is the opportunity for self-reflection and growth. When individuals take the time to identify areas in their lives that need improvement, they are more likely to gain insights into their strengths and weaknesses. This self-awareness can help individuals better understand themselves and make informed decisions about their personal development. By setting goals that align with their values and aspirations, individuals can work towards becoming the best version of themselves.

Setting personal development goals also provides a framework for success. By creating a roadmap for achieving desired outcomes, individuals can stay organized and on track towards their goals. This framework allows individuals to prioritize tasks, allocate resources effectively, and overcome obstacles that may arise along the way. By setting realistic timelines and holding themselves accountable for their progress, individuals can increase their chances of success and achieve their personal development goals.

In order to set effective personal development goals, individuals should follow a few key steps. First, it is important to identify areas in their lives that they would like to improve. This could include areas such as career advancement, improving interpersonal relationships, or achieving better work-life balance. Once individuals have identified areas of focus, they can begin to set specific and measurable goals that align with their aspirations.

When setting personal development goals, it is important to ensure that they are SMART - specific, measurable, achievable, relevant, and time-bound. Specific goals are clear and well-defined, making it easier for individuals to track their progress and stay focused on their objectives. Measurable goals allow individuals to quantify their progress and determine whether they are on track to achieving their desired outcomes. Achievable goals are realistic and attainable, taking into account individual strengths and limitations. Relevant goals are aligned with individuals' values and aspirations, ensuring that they are meaningful and impactful. Time-bound goals have a deadline for completion, providing a sense of urgency and motivation to work towards achieving them.

Once individuals have set their personal development goals, it is important to create a plan of action for achieving them. This plan should outline the steps needed to reach each goal, including resources needed, potential obstacles, and strategies for overcoming challenges. By breaking down larger objectives into smaller tasks, individuals can create a roadmap for success and track their progress along the way.

In addition to creating a plan of action, individuals should also regularly review their progress towards their personal development goals. This could involve setting regular checkpoints to assess progress, adjusting goals as needed, and celebrating achievements along the way. By regularly reviewing and updating their goals, individuals can stay motivated and on track towards their desired outcomes. By identifying areas in their lives that need improvement, setting specific and measurable goals, and creating a plan of action, individuals can work towards becoming the best version of themselves. Through self-reflection, self-awareness, and determination, individuals can achieve their personal development goals and lead more fulfilling and successful lives.

Chapter 10: Overcoming Challenges and Adversity

- STRATEGIES FOR RESILIENCE and Perseverance

Resilience and perseverance are crucial qualities that can greatly impact an individual's ability to navigate through life's challenges and adversities. In the face of setbacks and obstacles, it is important to develop effective strategies that can help one bounce back and continue moving forward. This essay aims to explore various strategies for resilience and perseverance that individuals can employ to enhance their ability to overcome adversity and succeed in the face of challenges.

One key strategy for resilience and perseverance is developing a positive mindset. Optimism and a positive outlook can help individuals see challenges as opportunities for growth and learning, rather than insurmountable obstacles. By focusing on the silver lining and maintaining a hopeful attitude, individuals can build the mental fortitude needed to persevere through difficult times. Additionally, practicing gratitude and mindfulness can help individuals stay present and appreciate the positives in their lives, even when faced with adversity.

Another important strategy for resilience and perseverance is building a strong support network. Having a supportive community of family, friends, mentors, and colleagues can provide individuals with the emotional support, guidance, and encouragement needed to weather the storms of life. When faced with challenges, reaching out to others for help and support can help individuals feel less alone and more capable of overcoming obstacles. Moreover, having a strong support network can also provide individuals with valuable perspectives and insights that can help them navigate challenges more effectively.

Furthermore, developing adaptive coping strategies is essential for building resilience and perseverance. Instead of reacting impulsively or letting emotions take over, individuals can benefit from learning to regulate their emotions and respond to challenges in a more constructive manner. Techniques such as deep breathing, mindfulness meditation, and cognitive reframing can help individuals manage stress and negative emotions, allowing them to approach challenges with a clearer and more rational mindset. By developing healthy coping mechanisms, individuals can build the resilience needed to bounce back from setbacks and continue moving forward.

In addition, setting realistic goals and breaking them down into manageable steps can help individuals build resilience and perseverance. By creating a roadmap for success and celebrating small victories along the way, individuals can maintain a sense of progress and accomplishment, even in the face of setbacks. Moreover, setting specific, measurable, achievable, relevant, and time-bound (SMART) goals can help individuals stay focused and motivated, even when faced with challenges. By breaking down larger goals into smaller, achievable milestones, individuals can build momentum and resilience, ultimately making progress towards their desired outcomes.

Moreover, practicing self-care and prioritizing physical and mental well-being are essential components of building resilience and perseverance. Taking care of one's health through regular exercise, nutritious diet, and sufficient sleep can help individuals build the physical stamina needed to navigate challenges and setbacks. Additionally, engaging in activities that bring joy and fulfillment, such as hobbies, creative pursuits, or spending time with loved ones, can help individuals recharge and replenish their energy reserves. By prioritizing self-care and well-being, individuals can build the resilience needed to overcome adversity and persevere in the face of challenges. By developing a positive mindset, building a strong support network, implementing adaptive coping strategies, setting realistic goals, and prioritizing self-care, individuals can enhance their ability to bounce back from adversity and continue moving forward. Ultimately, by cultivating these strategies for resilience and perseverance, individuals can build the mental fortitude needed to overcome obstacles and achieve success in the face of challenges.

- Dealing with Stress and Pressure

In today's fast-paced and competitive world, it is inevitable that we will encounter stress and pressure in our lives. Whether it be at work, in school, or in our personal lives, stress and pressure can take a toll on our mental and physical well-being. It is important to understand how to effectively deal with these challenges in order to maintain a healthy and balanced lifestyle.

One of the first steps in managing stress and pressure is to recognize the signs and symptoms of these conditions. It is essential to be aware of how stress and pressure manifest themselves in our lives, as this can help us identify when we need to take action. Common symptoms of stress and pressure include feelings of overwhelm, irritability, fatigue, and difficulty concentrating. Physical symptoms such as headaches, stomachaches, and muscle tension are also common indicators of stress and pressure.

Once we have identified the signs of stress and pressure, it is important to take proactive steps to address these issues. This may involve setting boundaries in our personal and professional lives, prioritizing tasks, and practicing self-care activities such as exercise, meditation, or spending time with loved ones. It is crucial to find healthy coping mechanisms that work for us individually, as what works for one person may not work for another.

In addition to individual coping strategies, it can be helpful to seek support from others when dealing with stress and pressure. This may involve talking to a trusted friend, family member, or mental health professional about our feelings and experiences. Sometimes simply sharing our struggles with someone else can provide a sense of relief and validation. Support groups and online forums can also be valuable resources for connecting with others who are going through similar challenges.

Another important aspect of managing stress and pressure is maintaining a healthy work-life balance. It is easy to become consumed by our professional responsibilities and neglect our personal lives, but this can lead to burnout and increased stress. Setting boundaries around work hours, taking regular breaks, and prioritizing activities that bring us joy and relaxation are all important aspects of maintaining a healthy balance.

To summarize, it is important to remember that stress and pressure are a normal part of life and that it is okay to ask for help when needed. It is not a sign of weakness to seek support from others or to take time for ourselves to recharge. By addressing stress and pressure head-on and developing healthy coping mechanisms, we can better navigate the challenges that come our way and live a more fulfilling and balanced life.

- Turning Obstacles into Opportunities

Obstacles are an inevitable part of life, and the way we choose to approach and overcome them can significantly impact our personal and professional growth. Instead of viewing obstacles as barriers to success, we can choose to see them as opportunities for growth and development. By shifting our perspective, we can transform challenges into stepping stones towards achieving our goals.

One key strategy for turning obstacles into opportunities is to adopt a growth mindset. This mindset, popularized by psychologist Carol Dweck, is characterized by a belief that our abilities and intelligence can be developed through effort and perseverance. When faced with obstacles, individuals with a growth mindset are more likely to see them as temporary setbacks that can be overcome with hard work and determination. By cultivating a growth mindset, we can reframe obstacles as opportunities to learn new skills, build resilience, and ultimately achieve greater success.

Another important factor in turning obstacles into opportunities is the ability to adapt and be flexible in the face of challenges. In today's rapidly changing world, the ability to pivot and adjust our approach when faced with obstacles is crucial for success. By embracing change and being open to new possibilities, we can uncover hidden opportunities that may not have been apparent initially. By staying adaptable and resilient, we can navigate obstacles with grace and come out stronger on the other side.

Furthermore, developing problem-solving skills is essential for turning obstacles into opportunities. When faced with a challenge, it's important to approach it systematically and strategically. By breaking down the obstacle into manageable steps and exploring different solutions, we can find creative ways to overcome it. Problem-solving skills not only help us tackle obstacles head-on but also enable us to think critically and innovatively in the face of adversity.

Additionally, building a strong support network can be instrumental in turning obstacles into opportunities. Surrounding ourselves with positive, like-minded individuals who offer encouragement, guidance, and support can help us navigate challenges more effectively. By seeking advice and feedback from trusted mentors, colleagues, and friends, we can gain valuable insights and perspectives that can help us overcome obstacles with confidence and resilience. By embracing challenges as opportunities for growth and development, we can navigate obstacles with confidence and resilience. With determination and perseverance, we can transform setbacks into stepping stones towards achieving our goals and ultimately realizing our full potential. So, the next time you encounter an obstacle, remember to approach it with a positive mindset, adaptability, problem-solving skills, and a strong support network. Together, these strategies can help you turn obstacles into opportunities and propel you towards success in all areas of your life.

Chapter 11: Finding Your Passion and Purpose

- DISCOVERING WHAT MOTIVATES You

Discovering what motivates you is a critical step in achieving success and fulfillment in both your personal and professional life. Understanding your core motivators can help you make decisions that align with your values, goals, and passions. By uncovering what drives you, you can tap into a powerful source of energy and determination that can propel you forward towards achieving your dreams.

One of the first steps in discovering what motivates you is to reflect on your past experiences and identify moments where you felt truly inspired and driven. Think about the times when you were engaged in an activity or pursuing a goal, and you felt a sense of purpose and fulfillment. What were the factors that contributed to your motivation in those moments. Was it the sense of accomplishment, the desire to make a difference, or the thrill of overcoming challenges. By examining these experiences, you can start to gain insight into what truly motivates you at a deep level.

Another important aspect of discovering your motivators is to consider your values and beliefs. What is important to you in life. What principles do you hold dear. Your values can serve as a compass that guides your decisions and actions. When your goals and actions are aligned with your values, you will feel a sense of congruence and authenticity that fuels your motivation. Take some time to reflect on what matters most to you and how your values can shape your goals and aspirations.

Self-awareness is a key component of understanding your motivators. By paying attention to your emotions, thoughts, and behaviors, you can gain valuable insights into what drives you. Notice when you feel excited, engaged, and energized in different situations. What are the common themes or patterns that emerge. This awareness can help you pinpoint the factors that ignite your passion and fuel your motivation. By tuning into your inner thoughts and feelings, you can uncover the deeper reasons behind your actions and decisions.

It can also be helpful to explore your strengths and weaknesses in relation to your motivators. What are the skills and talents that come naturally to you. How do these strengths align with your core motivations. By leveraging your strengths in pursuit of your goals, you can increase your chances of success and fulfillment. On the other hand, being aware of your weaknesses can help you identify areas for growth and development. By addressing these challenges, you can enhance your motivation and resilience in the face of obstacles.

Setting meaningful goals is an essential part of harnessing your motivation. When you have a clear sense of purpose and direction, you are more likely to stay focused and committed to achieving your objectives. Take the time to define your short-term and long-term goals, and consider how they align with your core motivators. Make sure your goals are SMART - specific, measurable, achievable, relevant, and time-bound. By breaking down your goals into manageable steps, you can create a roadmap for success that keeps you motivated and on track.

In addition to setting goals, it is important to cultivate a growth mindset that embraces challenges and setbacks as opportunities for learning and growth. When you approach obstacles with a positive attitude and a willingness to learn from your experiences, you can bounce back stronger and more motivated than ever. Remember that failure is not a reflection of your worth or abilities, but a natural part of the learning process. By cultivating resilience and perseverance, you can overcome setbacks and continue to pursue your goals with determination and courage.

Seeking feedback and support from others can also help you uncover what motivates you. Take the time to talk to friends, family members, mentors, and colleagues about your goals and aspirations. Listen to their perspectives and insights on what they see as your strengths, values, and motivators. Their feedback can offer valuable perspective and guidance that can help you gain clarity on what drives you. Surround yourself with people who support and encourage your growth and development, and seek out opportunities to learn from their experiences and wisdom. By reflecting on your past experiences, values, strengths, goals, and feedback from others, you can gain valuable insights into what drives you at a deep level. By aligning your actions and decisions with your core motivators, you can tap into a powerful source of energy and determination that empowers you to pursue your dreams with passion and conviction. Remember that motivation is a dynamic and evolving process that requires ongoing reflection, self-awareness, and growth. Embrace the journey of discovering what motivates you, and embrace the power within you to create a life filled with purpose and meaning.

- Aligning Your Goals with Your Passions

Aligning your goals with your passions is a crucial aspect of achieving success and fulfillment in both your personal and professional life. When your goals are aligned with your passions, you are more likely to feel motivated, engaged, and inspired to work towards them. This alignment allows you to tap into your natural strengths, talents, and interests, leading to a more enjoyable and rewarding journey towards your goals.

One of the first steps in aligning your goals with your passions is to take the time to identify and reflect on what truly excites and motivates you. What activities do you find most fulfilling and enjoyable. What topics or subjects do you find yourself naturally drawn towards. These are the things that indicate where your passions lie. By acknowledging and embracing these passions, you can begin to set goals that are not only meaningful to you but also resonate with your core values and beliefs.

Once you have identified your passions, the next step is to set specific, measurable, achievable, relevant, and time-bound (SMART) goals that align with them. For example, if your passion is helping others, you may set a goal to volunteer at a local charity organization for a certain number of hours each week. By setting goals that are in line with your passions, you are more likely to stay focused, committed, and driven to achieve them.

It's important to remember that aligning your goals with your passions does not mean that every goal you set will be easy or without challenges. In fact, pursuing your passions often requires dedication, hard work, and perseverance. However, when you are truly passionate about something, you are more willing to put in the effort and overcome obstacles along the way. This intrinsic motivation can be a powerful driving force that propels you towards success.

Another benefit of aligning your goals with your passions is the sense of fulfillment and satisfaction that comes from pursuing something that truly matters to you. When you are passionate about your goals, you are more likely to experience a sense of purpose and meaning in your work. This can lead to increased happiness, confidence, and overall well-being. Additionally, aligning your goals with your passions can help you stay focused and motivated, even when faced with challenges or setbacks. Your passion can serve as a source of inspiration and resilience during difficult times, helping you push through and continue working towards your goals. By identifying your passions, setting SMART goals that align with them, and staying committed and dedicated to your pursuits, you can create a path that is both rewarding and meaningful. Remember that pursuing your passions may not always be easy, but the hard work and effort you put in will be well worth it in the end. Embrace your passions, set meaningful goals, and watch as you unlock your full potential and achieve your dreams.

- Creating a Vision for Your Future

Creating a vision for your future is an essential aspect of personal development and goal setting. By envisioning where you want to be in the future, you can create a roadmap to guide your actions and decisions. A clear vision provides focus and motivation, allowing you to set meaningful goals and work towards achieving them. In this article, we will explore the importance of creating a vision for your future and provide practical tips on how to develop a compelling vision that aligns with your values and aspirations.

First and foremost, creating a vision for your future requires introspection and self-reflection. Take time to assess your strengths, weaknesses, values, and goals. Consider what is important to you and what you want to achieve in the long term. Reflect on your passions, interests, and aspirations, and think about how you can leverage them to create a vision that excites and motivates you. By taking an honest and thoughtful inventory of yourself, you can identify what matters most to you and what you want to prioritize in your future endeavors.

Once you have a clear understanding of your values and aspirations, it is time to start crafting your vision for the future. Start by thinking about where you want to be in the next 5, 10, or 20 years. Paint a vivid picture in your mind of what your ideal future looks like – what are you doing, who are you with, and what impact are you making on the world. Imagine yourself living your best life, achieving your goals, and fulfilling your dreams. Visualize the possibilities and opportunities that lie ahead, and let yourself dream big.

When creating your vision for the future, it is essential to make it specific, actionable, and realistic. Set clear and measurable goals that align with your values and aspirations. Break down your vision into smaller milestones and objectives that you can work towards over time. Make a plan to achieve your goals, and identify the steps you need to take to move closer to your vision. By making your vision concrete and achievable, you can stay focused and motivated to work towards it.

In addition to setting specific goals, it is crucial to make your vision for the future flexible and adaptable. Life is unpredictable, and circumstances may change, so it is essential to be open to adjusting your vision as needed. Be willing to revise your goals and plans as you progress towards your vision, and be open to exploring new opportunities and possibilities that may arise. By staying flexible and adaptable, you can navigate challenges and setbacks more effectively and stay on course towards your desired future.

Another key aspect of creating a vision for your future is to surround yourself with a supportive network of friends, family, mentors, and peers who can help you achieve your goals. Share your vision with others and seek feedback and guidance from those who know you best. Seek advice from mentors and role models who have achieved success in their own lives, and learn from their experiences and insights. By building a strong support system, you can stay motivated and accountable for your actions, and receive the encouragement and guidance you need to stay on track towards your vision. By envisioning where you want to be in the future, you can set meaningful goals, stay focused and motivated, and make progress towards achieving your dreams. By taking the time to reflect on your values and aspirations, set specific and actionable goals, stay flexible and adaptable, and surround yourself with a supportive network, you can create a vision for your future that inspires and empowers you to live a fulfilling and meaningful life. So take the time to envision your ideal future, set goals that align with your values and passions,

and take the necessary steps to turn your vision into reality. Your future is in
your hands – make it count.

Chapter 12: Embracing Creativity and Innovation

- CULTIVATING CREATIVITY in Problem-Solving

Creativity is a key component in finding innovative solutions to complex problems. Cultivating creativity in problem-solving requires a combination of skills, mindset, and practices. The first step in fostering creativity is to embrace a growth mindset. This mindset encourages individuals to believe that their abilities can be developed through dedication and hard work. By viewing challenges as opportunities for growth, individuals are more likely to think outside the box and come up with creative solutions.

Additionally, exposure to diverse experiences and perspectives can enrich one's creative thinking. By engaging with different cultures, disciplines, and ways of thinking, individuals can expand their creative capacities and generate new ideas. Collaborating with others who have different backgrounds and expertise can also spark creativity by bringing together a variety of perspectives and approaches to problem-solving.

Incorporating creative practices into one's routine can also help cultivate creativity in problem-solving. Activities such as brainstorming, mind mapping, and visualization can help individuals generate new ideas and explore different possibilities. Experimenting with different techniques and tools can also stimulate creativity and help individuals think more creatively about solutions to complex problems.

Furthermore, creating a supportive and inclusive environment is essential for fostering creativity in problem-solving. By encouraging risk-taking, valuing diverse perspectives, and providing opportunities for collaboration, organizations can create a culture that nurtures creativity. Recognizing and rewarding creative thinking can also motivate individuals to think more creatively and approach problems from unique angles. By embracing a growth mindset, exposing oneself to diverse experiences and perspectives, incorporating creative practices into one's routine, and creating a supportive and inclusive environment, individuals can enhance their creative thinking and generate innovative solutions to complex problems. By fostering creativity in problem-solving, individuals and organizations can stay ahead of the curve and adapt to changing circumstances with agility and effectiveness.

- Embracing Change and Adaptability

Change is an inevitable and constant aspect of life that impacts individuals, organizations, and societies at large. In today's fast-paced and dynamic world, the ability to adapt to change is crucial for personal growth and success. Embracing change and being adaptable allows individuals to navigate uncertain and challenging situations with resilience and flexibility. This mindset not only promotes creativity and innovation but also fosters a culture of continuous learning and development.

One of the key reasons why embracing change is important is because it enables individuals to stay relevant and competitive in a rapidly evolving world. The ability to adapt to new technologies, trends, and ways of working is essential for success in today's interconnected and digital age. By staying open to change and being willing to learn and grow, individuals can position themselves as valuable assets in their personal and professional lives. Embracing change can also lead to new opportunities and experiences that may not have been possible if one had resisted or avoided change.

Furthermore, embracing change and adaptability can foster personal growth and development. By stepping out of one's comfort zone and embracing new experiences, individuals can gain new skills, perspectives, and insights that can enrich their lives. Being adaptable allows individuals to be more resilient in the face of adversity and uncertainty, as they are better able to navigate challenges and setbacks with a positive attitude and growth mindset. This ability to adapt and evolve is key to personal and professional success in a rapidly changing world.

Additionally, embracing change can lead to increased creativity and innovation. When individuals are open to new ideas and ways of thinking, they are more likely to come up with creative solutions to complex problems. Embracing change allows individuals to experiment, take risks, and push the boundaries of what is possible. This mindset of creativity and innovation is essential for organizations looking to stay ahead of the competition and drive business growth. By fostering a culture of adaptability and change, organizations can encourage employees to think outside the box and come up with fresh ideas that can lead to breakthrough innovations. By staying open to new experiences, learning opportunities, and ways of working, individuals can position themselves for success and stay relevant in an ever-changing environment. Embracing change allows individuals to be more resilient, creative, and innovative, leading to personal development and growth. By fostering a culture of adaptability and change, organizations can drive business growth and stay ahead of the competition. Embracing change is not always easy, but it is a necessary mindset for success in a constantly evolving world.

- Thinking Outside the Box for Success

Thinking outside the box is a concept that has become increasingly popular in modern business and academic circles. It refers to the ability to approach problems and challenges in unconventional ways, often leading to innovative solutions and breakthrough discoveries. This mindset is essential for success in today's fast-paced and competitive world, where traditional methods and strategies are no longer sufficient to achieve desired outcomes. By thinking outside the box, individuals can tap into their creativity and find new ways to tackle complex problems, drive growth, and pave the way for success.

One of the key benefits of thinking outside the box is the ability to generate new ideas and solutions that may not have been considered through conventional thinking. This approach encourages individuals to break free from limitations and explore alternative perspectives, leading to fresh insights and innovative approaches. By challenging existing norms and exploring uncharted territory, individuals can uncover new opportunities and possibilities that may have been overlooked. This can result in groundbreaking innovations, competitive advantages, and transformative changes that propel individuals and organizations to success.

Furthermore, thinking outside the box fosters a culture of creativity and innovation within an organization. By encouraging employees to explore new ideas and approaches, organizations can tap into the diverse talents and perspectives of their workforce, driving collaboration and synergy. This can lead to a dynamic and forward-thinking environment where creativity is valued, ideas are nurtured, and innovation is a constant pursuit. By fostering a culture of creativity and innovation, organizations can stay ahead of the curve, adapt to changing market dynamics, and position themselves for sustained success in a rapidly evolving landscape.

In addition, thinking outside the box can help individuals and organizations navigate uncertainty and challenge the status quo. In today's unpredictable and complex world, traditional solutions and strategies are often not enough to address the myriad of challenges that arise. By thinking outside the box, individuals can approach problems with a fresh perspective, adapt to changing circumstances, and find solutions that are agile and resilient. This flexibility and adaptability are essential for success in a rapidly changing world where the only constant is change.

Thinking outside the box also empowers individuals to take calculated risks and embrace failure as a learning opportunity. By exploring new ideas and approaches, individuals may encounter setbacks and obstacles along the way. However, these challenges can be viewed as valuable learning experiences that can lead to growth and improvement. By embracing failure as a natural part of the creative process, individuals can develop resilience, persistence, and a growth mindset that is essential for success. This willingness to take risks and learn from mistakes can lead to breakthrough discoveries, bold innovations, and unprecedented success that would not have been possible through conventional thinking.

Furthermore, thinking outside the box can lead to increased personal and professional satisfaction. By embracing creativity and innovation, individuals can find fulfillment in their work, pursue their passions, and make a meaningful impact in their organizations and communities. This sense of purpose and fulfillment can drive motivation, engagement, and productivity, leading to greater success and satisfaction in all aspects of life. By thinking outside the box and pursuing unconventional paths, individuals can unlock their full potential, achieve their goals, and create a legacy that resonates far beyond their own lifetime. By embracing creativity, innovation, and a willingness to challenge the status quo, individuals can unlock new possibilities, drive growth, and achieve breakthrough success. Thinking outside the box empowers individuals to approach problems with fresh perspectives, spark creativity, and find new solutions that are agile and resilient. This mindset fosters a culture of creativity and innovation within organizations, leading to collaboration, synergy, and transformative changes. By taking calculated risks, embracing failure as a learning opportunity, and pursuing personal and professional fulfillment, individuals can unlock their full potential and create a lasting impact that resonates far beyond their own lifetime. Thinking outside the box is not just a mindset, but a way of life that can lead to unprecedented success and fulfillment for individuals and organizations alike.

Chapter 13: Managing Finances and Resources

- BUDGETING AND FINANCIAL Planning

Budgeting and financial planning are essential components of personal and professional financial management. A budget is a detailed plan that outlines income and expenses over a specific period, typically on a monthly or annual basis. Financial planning, on the other hand, is a broader process that encompasses setting financial goals, creating a budget, saving, investing, and managing debt. Both budgeting and financial planning are crucial for achieving long-term financial stability and success.

Creating and sticking to a budget is key to achieving financial goals and managing expenses effectively. A budget helps individuals and organizations track their spending, identify areas where they can cut costs or increase savings, and prioritize their financial goals. By setting realistic goals and tracking progress regularly, individuals can make informed decisions about their finances and stay on track to achieve their objectives. Additionally, a budget can help individuals avoid overspending, accumulate savings, and prepare for unexpected expenses.

Financial planning involves setting short-term and long-term financial goals, creating a budget to achieve those goals, and implementing strategies to reach them. Financial planning also includes saving for retirement, investing for the future, managing debt, and protecting assets through insurance. By developing a comprehensive financial plan, individuals can ensure that they are prepared for major life events, such as buying a home, getting married, starting a family, or retiring.

Budgeting and financial planning are interconnected, as a budget is a tool used in the financial planning process. A budget helps individuals allocate their resources effectively and make informed decisions about spending, saving, and investing. By creating a budget as part of their financial plan, individuals can ensure that they are on track to achieve their financial goals and maintain financial stability over the long term. A well-thought-out financial plan can help individuals navigate life's financial challenges and achieve their dreams.

There are several key steps to creating a budget and financial plan. The first step is to set clear financial goals, such as saving for a down payment on a house, paying off debt, or retiring comfortably. Once goals are established, individuals can create a budget that outlines their income, expenses, and savings targets. It is important to be realistic when setting financial goals and budgeting, as unrealistic goals can lead to frustration and failure. By setting achievable goals and creating a budget that aligns with those goals, individuals can stay motivated and make progress towards their financial objectives.

Once a budget is in place, it is essential to track spending and adjust as needed. Regularly monitoring expenses and comparing them to the budget can help individuals identify areas where they are overspending, as well as opportunities to save money or increase income. By reviewing the budget regularly and making adjustments as needed, individuals can stay on track to achieve their financial goals. Additionally, tracking expenses can help individuals identify patterns in their spending habits and make informed decisions about where to cut costs or reallocate funds.

In addition to creating a budget, individuals should also consider the role of saving and investing in their financial plan. Saving money is an essential component of financial planning, as it allows individuals to build an emergency fund, save for major expenses, and plan for retirement. By setting aside a portion of income each month for savings, individuals can build a financial cushion and prepare for unexpected expenses. Investing is another important aspect of financial planning, as it allows individuals to grow their wealth and achieve long-term financial goals. By diversifying investments and seeking professional advice, individuals can make informed decisions about where to invest their money and achieve their financial goals.

Managing debt is another critical aspect of financial planning. Debt can be a significant obstacle to achieving financial goals and can lead to financial stress and uncertainty. By creating a plan to pay off debt, individuals can reduce financial burdens, improve their credit score, and free up funds for saving and investing. By prioritizing high-interest debt and making regular payments, individuals can make progress towards becoming debt-free and achieving financial independence. By creating a budget, setting financial goals, saving, investing, and managing debt, individuals can make informed decisions about their finances and stay on track to achieve their objectives. By developing a comprehensive financial plan that includes a budget, individuals can navigate life's financial challenges, build wealth, and achieve their dreams. By setting clear financial goals, creating a budget that aligns with those goals, and implementing strategies to achieve them, individuals can take control of their finances and secure their financial future.

- Investing in Your Future

Investing in your future is a crucial aspect of personal finance that involves making wise decisions today in order to secure a better tomorrow. Whether you are just starting out in your career or are well-established in your profession, taking the time to plan and strategize for your future financial well-being is essential. By making thoughtful and informed choices about how you save, spend, and invest your money, you can build a solid foundation for long-term financial success and stability. In this essay, we will delve into the various ways in which you can invest in your future, from setting financial goals to creating a diversified investment portfolio.

One of the first steps in investing in your future is to establish clear financial goals. These goals can vary widely depending on your age, income level, and personal circumstances, but they should always be realistic, measurable, and time-bound. For example, if your goal is to retire comfortably at the age of 65, you may need to calculate how much money you will need to save each month in order to reach that goal. By setting specific targets and timelines for achieving your financial objectives, you can stay motivated and on track to meet your long-term goals.

In addition to setting clear financial goals, it is important to create a budget that aligns with your objectives. A budget is a detailed plan that outlines your income, expenses, and savings goals on a monthly basis. By tracking your spending and income, you can identify areas where you may be overspending and find opportunities to cut costs and increase your savings. Developing a budget can also help you avoid the pitfalls of living beyond your means and accumulating debt, which can derail your efforts to invest in your future.

Once you have established your financial goals and created a budget, the next step in investing in your future is to start building an emergency fund. An emergency fund is a savings account that is specifically set aside to cover unexpected expenses, such as medical bills, car repairs, or job loss. By having a financial cushion in place, you can avoid dipping into your long-term investments or going into debt when an unexpected expense arises. Most financial experts recommend saving at least three to six months' worth of living expenses in an emergency fund to provide a sufficient safety net in case of a financial setback.

After you have built an emergency fund, the next step in investing in your future is to start saving for retirement. Saving for retirement is a long-term goal that requires careful planning and consistent contributions to a retirement account, such as a 401(k) or an individual retirement account (IRA). By starting to save for retirement early and regularly, you can take advantage of the power of compound interest, which allows your investments to grow over time. In addition to saving for retirement, it is also important to consider factors such as inflation, taxes, and healthcare costs when planning for your future financial needs.

In addition to saving for retirement, investing in your future also involves creating a diversified investment portfolio that aligns with your risk tolerance and investment objectives. A diversified portfolio is a mix of different asset classes, such as stocks, bonds, real estate, and mutual funds, that can help reduce the overall risk of your investments and maximize potential returns. By diversifying your investments across different asset classes and industries, you can spread out risk and increase the likelihood of achieving your financial goals over the long term. It is important to regularly review and rebalance your investment portfolio to ensure that it remains aligned with your financial goals and risk tolerance.

Another important aspect of investing in your future is to consider the impact of taxes on your investments and financial planning. Taxes can significantly affect the after-tax returns of your investments, so it is important to understand how different types of investments are taxed and to develop strategies to minimize your tax liabilities. For example, investing in tax-advantaged accounts, such as a Roth IRA or a health savings account (HSA), can help you save on taxes and potentially increase your investment returns over time. Working with a qualified financial advisor or tax professional can also help you navigate the complex tax laws and optimize your investment strategy for tax efficiency. By taking the time to plan and strategize for your future financial well-being, you can lay the groundwork for long-term financial success and stability. While the prospect of investing in your future may seem overwhelming at times, it is important to take small and consistent steps towards your financial goals in order to achieve lasting financial security and peace of mind. By making informed decisions and staying disciplined in your financial planning, you can build a solid foundation for a brighter and more secure future.

- Maximizing Your Resources for Success

Maximizing your resources for success is a crucial aspect of achieving your goals and reaching your full potential. Whether you are a student, a professional, or an entrepreneur, the ability to effectively utilize the resources available to you can make a significant difference in your success. Resources can come in many forms, including time, money, skills, and connections. By leveraging these resources effectively, you can increase your productivity, efficiency, and overall success.

One key aspect of maximizing your resources for success is proper time management. Time is a finite resource, and how you choose to allocate your time can have a significant impact on your success. By prioritizing tasks, setting goals, and creating a schedule, you can ensure that you are making the most of your time and focusing on the activities that will help you reach your objectives. Avoiding procrastination and staying organized can also help you make the most of your time and increase your productivity.

Another important resource to consider is money. Whether you are a student managing a tight budget, an entrepreneur seeking funding for a new venture, or a professional looking to invest in your career development, managing your finances wisely is crucial for success. By creating a budget, setting financial goals, and being mindful of your spending habits, you can make the most of your financial resources and ensure that you are working towards your long-term goals.

Skills and knowledge are also valuable resources that can help you succeed in your endeavors. By continuously learning, expanding your skill set, and staying up-to-date on the latest developments in your field, you can position yourself for success and increase your marketability. Whether through formal education, on-the-job training, or self-study, investing in your skills and knowledge can pay off in the form of career advancement, new opportunities, and personal growth.

Lastly, connections and relationships are a valuable resource that can help you succeed in your professional and personal life. By building a strong network of contacts, mentors, and supporters, you can access valuable advice, opportunities, and resources that can help you achieve your goals. Networking, attending industry events, and seeking out mentorship opportunities are all ways to cultivate meaningful connections that can contribute to your success. By prioritizing time management, financial planning, skill development, and relationship-building, you can position yourself for success and achieve your goals. Whether you are a student, a professional, or an entrepreneur, leveraging your resources effectively can help you reach your full potential and make the most of your opportunities. By being proactive, disciplined, and focused, you can make the most of the resources available to you and set yourself up for success in all areas of your life.

Chapter 14: Health and Wellness for Success

- THE LINK BETWEEN HEALTH and Productivity

Productivity is a key factor in the success of any organization, as it directly impacts the efficiency and effectiveness of the workforce. One often overlooked aspect that can have a significant impact on productivity is the health of employees. Research has shown that there is a strong link between health and productivity, with healthy individuals being more likely to perform better at work. This connection has important implications for employers, as fostering a healthy work environment can lead to improved performance and ultimately increased profitability.

Numerous studies have demonstrated the positive relationship between employee health and productivity. For example, a study published in the Journal of Occupational and Environmental Medicine found that employees who engaged in regular physical activity were more productive at work compared to their sedentary counterparts. Similarly, research has shown that individuals who have a healthy diet and get an adequate amount of sleep are more likely to perform well at work. These findings highlight the importance of promoting healthy lifestyle choices among employees as a means of enhancing productivity in the workplace.

One of the key reasons why health is linked to productivity is the impact that physical and mental well-being can have on an individual's ability to focus and concentrate. When employees are in good physical health, they are less likely to experience fatigue and are better able to sustain their attention on tasks. Likewise, individuals who are mentally healthy are more likely to have a positive outlook and be more engaged in their work. By prioritizing the health of employees, organizations can create a work environment that supports optimal performance and productivity.

Another important factor to consider in the link between health and productivity is the role that stress plays in the workplace. Chronic stress can have a significant negative impact on both physical and mental health, leading to decreased productivity and increased absenteeism. By implementing strategies to reduce stress and promote well-being, employers can help employees better cope with the demands of their job and improve their overall performance. This may include offering wellness programs, flexible work arrangements, and access to mental health resources.

In addition to the benefits for employees, there are also economic reasons for employers to invest in the health of their workforce. A study conducted by the World Health Organization found that for every dollar invested in workplace wellness programs, there was a return of $3. 27 in improved productivity and decreased healthcare costs. This underscores the value of implementing initiatives to promote employee health as a means of enhancing organizational performance and profitability. By prioritizing the well-being of employees, employers can create a positive work culture that fosters a healthy and productive workforce. By promoting a healthy work environment, employers can improve the physical and mental well-being of employees, leading to increased focus, engagement, and performance. Investing in workplace wellness programs and initiatives not only benefits employees but also has positive economic outcomes for organizations. Ultimately, the connection between health and productivity underscores the importance of prioritizing the well-being of employees in order to create a successful and thriving work environment.

- Prioritizing Self-Care and Well-Being

In today's fast-paced and demanding world, it is easy to prioritize work, deadlines, and responsibilities over our own well-being. However, it is crucial to understand the importance of prioritizing self-care and well-being in order to lead a more balanced and fulfilling life. Self-care is not selfish or indulgent; it is a fundamental aspect of maintaining physical, mental, and emotional health. By making self-care a priority, we can enhance our overall quality of life and promote a sense of well-being that can positively impact all aspects of our daily lives.

Self-care encompasses a wide range of practices and activities that are aimed at nourishing and nurturing our physical, emotional, and mental well-being. This can include activities such as exercise, meditation, healthy eating, spending time with loved ones, engaging in hobbies, and practicing mindfulness. These practices are not just luxuries or optional activities; they are essential for maintaining balance and managing stress in our lives. When we neglect self-care, we can experience negative consequences such as burnout, fatigue, anxiety, and depression. By prioritizing self-care, we can prevent these negative outcomes and instead promote a sense of well-being and resilience in the face of life's challenges.

One of the first steps in prioritizing self-care is recognizing the importance of taking care of ourselves. It is easy to fall into the trap of believing that we must always put others' needs before our own or that self-care is selfish or indulgent. However, this mindset is not only harmful to ourselves but can also prevent us from being able to effectively care for others. By prioritizing self-care, we can replenish our physical, emotional, and mental resources so that we are better able to show up fully for others in our lives. This is not a self-serving act, but rather an essential practice that allows us to be our best selves and support those around us.

Another important aspect of prioritizing self-care is setting boundaries and recognizing our own limits. It is easy to fall into the trap of overcommitting ourselves or saying yes to every request that comes our way. However, this can quickly lead to burnout and exhaustion, making it impossible to effectively care for ourselves or others. By setting boundaries and learning to say no when necessary, we can ensure that we are able to prioritize our own well-being and prevent ourselves from becoming overwhelmed. This can be a difficult practice to implement, especially for those who are used to putting others' needs before their own. However, by recognizing our own limits and learning to prioritize self-care, we can create a more balanced and fulfilling life for ourselves and those around us.

In addition to setting boundaries and recognizing our limits, another important aspect of prioritizing self-care is making time for activities that nourish and replenish us. This can include engaging in activities that bring us joy, spending time with loved ones, or engaging in mindfulness practices that promote relaxation and stress relief. These activities may seem simple or even trivial, but they are essential for maintaining balance and well-being in our lives. By making time for self-care activities, we can prevent burnout, reduce stress, and promote a sense of overall well-being that can positively impact all areas of our lives.

It is also important to remember that self-care is not a one-size-fits-all practice. What works for one person may not work for another, so it is essential to experiment with different self-care activities and practices to find what works best for you. This may require some trial and error, but the important thing is to listen to your body and mind and prioritize activities that help you feel nourished, replenished, and revitalized. Whether it is through exercise, meditation, spending time in nature, or engaging in creative activities, there are countless ways to prioritize self-care and well-being in your daily life. By recognizing the importance of self-care, setting boundaries, making time for nourishing activities, and experimenting with different practices, we can promote a sense of well-being and fulfillment in our lives. Self-care is not an optional luxury; it is an essential practice that allows us to show up fully for ourselves and others. By making self-care a priority, we can prevent burnout, reduce stress, and create a more balanced and fulfilling life for ourselves and those around us.

- Balancing Work and Personal Life

Balancing work and personal life is a critical aspect of maintaining overall well-being and achieving success in both areas. In today's fast-paced and demanding world, it can be challenging to find the right balance between fulfilling work responsibilities and spending quality time with loved ones, pursuing personal interests, and taking care of oneself. However, with careful planning, effective time management, and proactive communication, individuals can strive for harmony between their professional and personal lives.

One key strategy for balancing work and personal life is setting clear boundaries and priorities. It is essential to establish limits on how much time and energy you devote to work activities and to be intentional about carving out time for personal activities and relationships. This may involve creating a schedule that includes dedicated time for work, relaxation, exercise, family time, and hobbies. By clearly defining your priorities and boundaries, you can prevent work from encroaching on your personal life and ensure that you are able to give sufficient attention to all areas of your life.

Effective time management is another crucial skill for achieving a healthy work-life balance. This includes prioritizing tasks, setting realistic goals, and avoiding distractions that can impede productivity. By identifying the most important tasks and focusing on completing them efficiently, you can free up time for personal activities and reduce stress levels. Additionally, utilizing tools such as calendars, to-do lists, and time-tracking apps can help you stay organized and ensure that you are making the most of your time.

Communication is also key to balancing work and personal life. It is important to communicate openly with your employer, colleagues, and loved ones about your commitments, boundaries, and needs. By setting expectations with your employer about your availability outside of work hours and discussing flexible work arrangements, you can create a more accommodating work environment that allows you to prioritize personal obligations. Similarly, maintaining open lines of communication with your family and friends can help ensure that everyone is on the same page about your availability and commitments, allowing for greater support and understanding.

Taking care of oneself is essential for achieving a healthy work-life balance. Self-care practices such as exercise, meditation, hobbies, and relaxation techniques can help reduce stress, improve mood, and increase overall well-being. By prioritizing self-care activities and making time for activities that bring joy and fulfillment, you can recharge and replenish your energy, making you more resilient and better equipped to handle the demands of work and personal life. Additionally, setting boundaries around work and avoiding overcommitting yourself can prevent burnout and ensure that you have the time and energy to invest in all aspects of your life. By setting clear boundaries, prioritizing tasks, communicating openly, and taking care of oneself, individuals can achieve a healthy work-life balance that allows them to excel in their professional roles while also enjoying a fulfilling personal life. Remember that achieving work-life balance is a journey, and it may require regular adjustments and fine-tuning to ensure that you are meeting your needs and achieving your goals. By cultivating a proactive and intentional approach to balancing work and personal life, you can create a fulfilling and harmonious life that reflects your values and priorities.

Chapter 15: Leadership and Influence

- DEVELOPING LEADERSHIP Skills

Developing leadership skills is an essential aspect of personal growth and professional success. A leader is someone who inspires and influences others to achieve common goals and objectives. With effective leadership skills, individuals can effectively manage teams, make informed decisions, and drive positive change within an organization. As such, there is a growing emphasis on the importance of developing leadership skills in both academic and professional settings.

One key aspect of developing leadership skills is understanding the various leadership styles and approaches. Different situations call for different leadership styles, and being able to adapt one's leadership approach to suit the needs of the team and the organization is crucial. Some common leadership styles include autocratic, democratic, transformational, and laissez-faire. A good leader understands when to be directive and when to be collaborative, when to inspire and motivate, and when to delegate responsibilities to others. By learning about these various leadership styles and approaches, individuals can become more versatile and effective leaders.

Another important aspect of developing leadership skills is improving communication and interpersonal skills. Effective communication is essential for building trust, motivating team members, and resolving conflicts. Leaders must be able to clearly articulate their vision, provide feedback, and listen actively to their team members. By honing their communication skills, leaders can create a positive work environment where ideas and feedback are shared openly and honestly. Additionally, strong interpersonal skills are also key to developing positive relationships with team members and stakeholders.

Leaders who are empathetic, approachable, and respectful inspire loyalty and commitment from their team members.

Furthermore, developing leadership skills also involves honing decision-making and problem-solving abilities. Leaders are faced with complex and often ambiguous situations that require quick and informed decisions. By cultivating critical thinking skills, leaders can analyze information, evaluate options, and make sound decisions that benefit the team and the organization as a whole. Problem-solving skills are also crucial for leaders to identify issues, develop solutions, and overcome challenges. By approaching problems with a solutions-oriented mindset, leaders can navigate obstacles and drive progress towards achieving organizational goals.

In addition to these technical skills, emotional intelligence is also a key component of effective leadership. Emotional intelligence, or the ability to understand and manage one's emotions and those of others, plays a significant role in building strong relationships, resolving conflicts, and motivating team members. Leaders with high emotional intelligence are able to empathize with others, communicate effectively, and remain calm under pressure. By developing emotional intelligence, leaders can create a positive and supportive work environment that fosters collaboration, innovation, and success.

In a nutshell, a crucial aspect of developing leadership skills is continuous learning and self-improvement. Leadership is a journey, not a destination, and the best leaders are lifelong learners who are open to feedback and willing to adapt to new challenges and opportunities. By seeking out mentorship, attending leadership development programs, and reading leadership literature, individuals can deepen their understanding of leadership principles and best practices. Additionally, self-reflection and self-awareness are also important for leaders to identify their strengths and weaknesses and work towards personal growth and improvement. By understanding different leadership styles, improving communication and interpersonal skills, honing decision-making and problem-solving abilities, developing emotional intelligence, and engaging in continuous learning and self-improvement, individuals can become effective and inspirational leaders who drive positive change within their organizations. Through dedication, perseverance, and a commitment to personal growth, individuals can develop the leadership skills necessary to succeed in today's dynamic and competitive business environment.

- Inspiring and Motivating Others

Inspiring and motivating others is a crucial skill in both professional and personal settings. Whether you are a leader in the workplace, a coach on a sports team, or a parent at home, the ability to inspire and motivate those around you can lead to increased productivity, improved morale, and stronger relationships. In this essay, we will discuss the importance of inspiring and motivating others, as well as some strategies for doing so effectively.

First and foremost, it is important to recognize that everyone is motivated by different things. Some people are driven by the desire for recognition and praise, while others are motivated by the opportunity to learn and grow. As a leader or influencer, it is important to take the time to understand what motivates each individual on your team or in your circle, so that you can tailor your approach accordingly. By taking the time to understand what drives each person, you can more effectively inspire and motivate them to achieve their goals.

In addition to understanding what motivates others, it is also important to lead by example. People are more likely to be inspired and motivated by someone who is passionate and dedicated to their own goals. By showing your own enthusiasm and commitment, you can inspire those around you to do the same. This can be as simple as setting ambitious goals for yourself and working diligently to achieve them, or as complex as demonstrating strong leadership skills in a challenging situation. Whatever the case may be, leading by example is a powerful way to inspire and motivate others.

Another important aspect of inspiring and motivating others is providing support and encouragement. People are more likely to be motivated to achieve their goals when they feel supported and encouraged by those around them. This can take many forms, from offering words of encouragement and praise, to providing resources and guidance to help someone succeed. By offering support and encouragement, you can help build confidence and self-esteem in others, which can lead to increased motivation and success.

One effective way to inspire and motivate others is to set clear goals and expectations. When people know what is expected of them and have a clear vision of what they are working towards, they are more likely to be motivated to achieve those goals. By setting specific, measurable, achievable, relevant, and time-bound (SMART) goals, you can provide a roadmap for success that can inspire and motivate others to accomplish their objectives. Additionally, by regularly reviewing progress and providing feedback, you can help keep people on track and motivated to reach their goals.

Communication is also a key component of inspiring and motivating others. By being open and transparent in your communication, you can build trust and credibility with those around you, which can lead to increased motivation and engagement. It is important to communicate clearly and consistently, providing information and feedback in a timely manner. Additionally, it is important to listen actively and empathetically to the concerns and ideas of others, so that you can better understand their motivations and needs. By fostering a culture of open communication, you can create an environment that is conducive to inspiring and motivating others.

Lastly, it is important to celebrate success and recognize the achievements of others. People are more likely to be motivated and inspired when they feel that their hard work and efforts are being acknowledged and appreciated. By taking the time to celebrate success and recognize the accomplishments of those around you, you can create a positive and supportive environment that encourages continued growth and success. This can take many forms, from small gestures of appreciation, to formal recognition programs and rewards. By making an effort to celebrate success, you can inspire and motivate others to reach their full potential. By taking the time to understand what motivates those around you, leading by example, providing support and encouragement, setting clear goals and expectations, communicating effectively, and celebrating success, you can create an environment that is conducive to inspiring and motivating others. By developing and honing these skills, you can become a more effective leader and influencer, capable of inspiring and motivating those around you to achieve their goals and succeed.

- Creating a Positive Impact in Your Community

Creating a positive impact in your community is a crucial aspect of being a responsible and engaged citizen. Whether you live in a small town or a bustling city, there are always opportunities to contribute to the well-being of those around you. By actively participating in community service, volunteering, and taking part in local initiatives, you can make a tangible difference in the lives of others and help foster a sense of unity and cooperation among community members.

One of the most effective ways to create a positive impact in your community is to get involved in local organizations and initiatives that address specific needs or issues in your area. This could include volunteering at a food bank, participating in a clean-up campaign, or joining a community garden project. By dedicating your time and energy to these causes, you can help provide essential services to those in need, improve the quality of life in your community, and build stronger connections with those around you.

In addition to participating in organized community efforts, you can also create a positive impact by simply being a good neighbor and lending a helping hand to those in your immediate vicinity. Whether it's offering to mow a neighbor's lawn, checking in on an elderly resident, or organizing a neighborhood watch group, small acts of kindness can go a long way in creating a sense of community and building trust among neighbors. By fostering a supportive and caring environment in your neighborhood, you can help prevent isolation and promote social cohesion among community members.

Another key component of creating a positive impact in your community is to actively engage with local government and advocate for positive change. This could involve attending town hall meetings, writing letters to elected officials, or joining local advocacy groups that work to address social, economic, or environmental issues in your area. By participating in the democratic process and voicing your concerns and suggestions, you can help influence policy decisions, improve public services, and promote greater transparency and accountability in local government.

Furthermore, creating a positive impact in your community also involves taking steps to promote diversity, equality, and inclusion among community members. By celebrating cultural differences, respecting individual identities, and advocating for social justice, you can help create a more inclusive and welcoming community that values and embraces the uniqueness of each resident. Promoting diversity and inclusion can help break down barriers, reduce prejudice and discrimination, and foster a sense of belonging and acceptance among community members.

Ultimately, creating a positive impact in your community requires a combination of individual effort, collective action, and a shared commitment to building a thriving and inclusive community for all. By actively engaging in community service, volunteering, advocating for positive change, and promoting diversity and inclusion, you can make a meaningful difference in the lives of those around you and contribute to the overall well-being and vitality of your community. Whether it's through participating in local initiatives, supporting neighbors in need, or voicing your concerns to elected officials, there are numerous ways you can make a positive impact and help create a stronger and more vibrant community for everyone.

Chapter 16: Building a Support System

- THE IMPORTANCE OF Surrounding Yourself with Positive Influences

In the complex world we live in, the people we surround ourselves with can have a profound impact on our lives and achievements. Positivity is contagious, and being around positive influences can elevate our mood, mindset, and overall well-being. Whether it be friends, family, colleagues, or mentors, surrounding ourselves with individuals who radiate positivity can inspire, motivate, and encourage us to strive for greatness. These positive influences can shape our beliefs, attitudes, and behaviors, ultimately leading to personal growth and success.

One of the key reasons why surrounding ourselves with positive influences is important is because it can significantly impact our mental health and emotional well-being. Positivity breeds happiness, and being around individuals who exude positivity can help reduce stress, anxiety, and negative emotions. When we are surrounded by positive influences, we are more likely to focus on the good in life, practice gratitude, and have a more optimistic outlook on the future. This positive mindset can help improve our overall mental health, increase our resilience in the face of challenges, and enhance our ability to cope with difficult situations.

Moreover, surrounding ourselves with positive influences can also have a profound impact on our personal development and growth. When we are surrounded by individuals who believe in our potential, support our goals, and encourage us to push past our limits, we are more likely to take risks, pursue our passions, and achieve our dreams. Positive influences can provide valuable feedback, guidance, and mentorship that can help us navigate the ups and downs of life with confidence and resilience. By surrounding ourselves with individuals who challenge us to be our best selves, we can unlock our full potential and tap into our inner strengths.

Furthermore, positive influences can help us cultivate healthy relationships and build a strong support system. Relationships play a vital role in our lives, and being surrounded by positive influences can help us foster deep connections based on trust, respect, and mutual support. Positive influences can offer encouragement, empathy, and understanding during tough times, and celebrate our successes and milestones with genuine joy and happiness. Having a strong support system of positive influences can provide us with a sense of belonging, security, and love that can help us navigate the complexities of life with grace and resilience.

In addition, surrounding ourselves with positive influences can also have a positive impact on our professional life and career. Positivity is a key trait of successful and effective leaders, and being around positive influences can help us develop the right mindset, attitude, and behaviors to excel in our careers. Positive influences can provide us with valuable insights, perspectives, and advice that can help us navigate the competitive world of work with confidence and resilience. By surrounding ourselves with individuals who believe in our capabilities, challenge us to grow, and support our career aspirations, we can enhance our professional development, build a strong network of allies and mentors, and achieve success in our chosen field. Positivity is a powerful force that can inspire, motivate, and empower us to overcome challenges, achieve our goals, and thrive in every aspect of our lives. By surrounding ourselves with individuals who radiate positivity, believe in our potential, and support our aspirations, we can cultivate a positive mindset, build healthy relationships, and excel in our personal and professional lives. So, let us choose our influences wisely, and surround ourselves with positivity, love, and support to create a life filled with happiness, success, and fulfillment.

- Fostering a Supportive Network of Relationships

In today's fast-paced and interconnected world, fostering a supportive network of relationships is more important than ever. Whether in our personal or professional lives, having a strong support system can make all the difference in achieving our goals and overcoming challenges. But what exactly does it mean to cultivate a supportive network of relationships, and how can we go about building and maintaining these important connections. In this essay, we will explore the various components of a supportive network, the benefits of having such a network, and some practical steps for building and nurturing relationships that can help us thrive in all areas of our lives.

At its core, a supportive network of relationships is comprised of individuals who provide emotional, psychological, and sometimes even physical support to each other. These relationships are characterized by mutual respect, trust, and empathy, and they serve as a source of strength and comfort in times of need. A supportive network can include friends, family members, colleagues, mentors, and even acquaintances who share common interests or goals. Each person in the network plays a unique role, offering different forms of support based on their individual strengths and expertise.

The benefits of having a supportive network of relationships are manifold. Research has shown that people with strong social connections are happier, healthier, and more resilient in the face of challenges. A supportive network can provide emotional support during difficult times, practical advice or assistance when needed, and a sense of belonging and camaraderie that can boost confidence and self-esteem. In the professional realm, a strong network can open doors to new opportunities, help advance careers, and provide valuable feedback and guidance that can lead to personal and professional growth. In short, a supportive network of relationships can be a valuable asset in both our personal and professional lives.

So how can we go about building and nurturing relationships that form a supportive network. One key aspect is to be open and proactive in seeking out new connections. This may involve attending networking events, joining professional or social organizations, or simply reaching out to colleagues or acquaintances who share common interests or goals. It's important to be genuine and authentic in building these relationships, as trust and mutual respect are essential for a supportive network to thrive. This means taking the time to get to know others on a deeper level, sharing our own experiences and vulnerabilities, and being willing to offer support and assistance in return.

Another important aspect of fostering a supportive network of relationships is communication. Healthy relationships are built on open and honest communication, so it's important to be transparent and upfront with others about our needs, boundaries, and expectations. This includes expressing gratitude and appreciation for the support we receive, as well as being willing to offer help and support to others in return. Effective communication also involves active listening, empathy, and understanding, as these qualities can help strengthen our relationships and build trust and rapport with others.

In addition to communication, it's important to prioritize self-care and set boundaries in our relationships. While having a supportive network can be incredibly valuable, it's also important to remember that we are individuals with our own needs and limitations. This means knowing when to ask for help and when to offer help, setting boundaries around our time and energy, and recognizing when a relationship may be toxic or draining. By prioritizing our own well-being and taking care of ourselves, we can ensure that we have the capacity to be a source of support for others in our network.

To culminate, building a supportive network of relationships requires ongoing effort and investment. It's important to nurture and maintain these relationships over time, through regular communication, participation in group activities, and showing up for others when they need us. This may involve reaching out to check in on a friend, attending a networking event, or offering to help a colleague with a project. By showing up consistently and being present for others, we can strengthen our relationships and ensure that our network remains supportive and resilient in the face of challenges. By building and nurturing relationships based on trust, empathy, and mutual respect, we can create a supportive network that provides emotional, practical, and professional support when we need it most. Through open and honest communication, setting boundaries, prioritizing self-care, and investing time and energy in our relationships, we can cultivate a network that helps us thrive in all areas of our lives. So let's make a conscious effort to build and maintain strong relationships that lift us up, inspire us, and help us become the best versions of ourselves.

- Seeking Mentors and Role Models for Guidance

Seeking mentors and role models for guidance is a crucial aspect of personal and professional development. Mentors are individuals who possess more experience and knowledge in a particular field or area of expertise and are willing to share their wisdom and insights with others. Role models, on the other hand, are inspiring figures who embody qualities and attributes that we admire and aspire to emulate. By seeking out mentors and role models, we can gain valuable guidance, support, and inspiration to help us navigate through challenges, make informed decisions, and achieve our goals.

One of the key benefits of having mentors and role models is the opportunity to learn from their experiences and expertise. Mentors can provide valuable advice, feedback, and perspective based on their own successes and failures. They can offer valuable insights and guidance on how to overcome obstacles, make strategic decisions, and navigate through complex situations. By tapping into their knowledge and expertise, we can avoid making common mistakes and learn from their proven strategies and practices. Role models, on the other hand, can inspire us to cultivate qualities such as integrity, resilience, and perseverance. By observing and learning from their behavior and actions, we can gain valuable insights on how to develop our own character, values, and leadership skills.

Another important benefit of seeking mentors and role models is the opportunity to expand our network and connect with like-minded individuals. Mentors and role models can introduce us to new ideas, opportunities, and resources that we may not have access to otherwise. They can provide valuable introductions and connections to other professionals, experts, and influencers in our industry or field. By building relationships with mentors and role models, we can cultivate a supportive network of advisors and allies who can provide valuable guidance, support, and encouragement as we navigate through our personal and professional journey.

Furthermore, mentors and role models can serve as a source of motivation and inspiration. They can encourage us to set high standards, push our limits, and strive for excellence in everything we do. By observing their achievements and accomplishments, we can envision what is possible and aspire to achieve similar levels of success and fulfillment. Mentors and role models can provide us with a sense of purpose and direction, guiding us towards our goals and dreams. Their belief in our potential and abilities can fuel our motivation and drive to overcome obstacles, persevere through challenges, and reach our full potential.

In addition to providing guidance and inspiration, mentors and role models can also offer emotional support and encouragement. They can serve as a sounding board for our ideas, thoughts, and concerns, providing a safe space for us to express ourselves openly and honestly. They can offer perspective and wisdom on how to manage stress, uncertainty, and self-doubt, helping us to build resilience and inner strength. Mentors and role models can provide a source of encouragement and validation, boosting our confidence and belief in ourselves. Their support and encouragement can help us to stay focused, motivated, and positive, even in the face of adversity and setbacks. Mentors and role models can provide valuable insights, advice, and perspective to help us navigate through challenges, make informed decisions, and achieve our goals. They can inspire us to cultivate qualities such as integrity, resilience, and perseverance, while also expanding our network and connecting us with like-minded individuals. Mentors and role models can serve as a source of motivation and inspiration, fueling our drive to overcome obstacles and reach our full potential. In addition, they can offer emotional support and encouragement, helping us to build resilience and inner strength. By seeking out mentors and role models, we can gain valuable guidance, support, and inspiration to help us succeed in our personal and professional lives.

Chapter 17: Adapting to Change and Uncertainty

- STRATEGIES FOR NAVIGATING Change Successfully

Change is an inevitable part of life, both personally and professionally. In today's constantly evolving world, organizations are faced with the challenge of navigating change successfully in order to stay competitive and relevant. It is essential for leaders and managers to develop effective strategies for managing change in order to minimize disruption and ensure a smooth transition process.

One of the key strategies for navigating change successfully is effective communication. It is important for leaders to clearly communicate the reasons for change, as well as the expected outcomes and benefits. Employees need to understand the rationale behind the change in order to buy into the process and actively participate in making it successful. Communication should be transparent and ongoing, with regular updates and opportunities for feedback to ensure that all stakeholders are kept informed and engaged throughout the change process.

Another important strategy for navigating change successfully is to involve employees in the decision-making process. When employees feel that their input is valued and that they have a say in the change process, they are more likely to be motivated and committed to making the change successful. Managers should create opportunities for employees to provide input, contribute ideas, and be part of the decision-making process. This not only helps to generate buy-in and support for the change, but also fosters a culture of collaboration and empowerment within the organization.

In addition to communication and employee involvement, it is crucial for leaders to provide support and resources to help employees adapt to change.

Change can be a stressful and challenging time for many employees, so it is important for managers to provide the necessary tools, training, and resources to help them navigate the change successfully. This may include offering training programs, coaching, mentoring, and other forms of support to help employees develop the skills and competencies needed to thrive in the new environment.

Furthermore, leaders should actively manage resistance to change in order to ensure a successful transition process. Resistance to change is a natural reaction to the unknown and the unfamiliar, but it can hinder the change process and prevent organizations from achieving their goals. It is important for leaders to be empathetic and understanding towards employees who may be resistant to change, and to address their concerns and fears in a constructive and supportive manner. By acknowledging and addressing resistance, leaders can help employees move past their fears and reservations and embrace the change with a positive attitude.

Lastly, it is important for leaders to celebrate success and recognize achievements throughout the change process. Change can be a long and arduous journey, and it is important to acknowledge and celebrate the small wins along the way. By recognizing and rewarding employees for their efforts and accomplishments, leaders can foster a sense of accomplishment and motivation within the organization, and create a positive and supportive environment for navigating change successfully. By implementing these strategies, leaders can help their organizations successfully navigate change and thrive in today's fast-paced and dynamic business environment. By fostering a culture of openness, collaboration, and innovation, organizations can adapt to change and drive growth and success in the long term.

- Embracing Uncertainty as an Opportunity for Growth

Uncertainty is a fundamental aspect of human existence. It permeates every aspect of our lives, from our personal relationships to our professional endeavors. While uncertainty can be uncomfortable and anxiety-inducing, it is also a powerful catalyst for growth and development. Embracing uncertainty as an opportunity for growth requires a shift in mindset and a willingness to embrace the unknown.

One of the key benefits of embracing uncertainty is the opportunity for personal growth and self-discovery. When we step outside of our comfort zones and face the unknown, we are forced to confront our fears and insecurities. This process of self-exploration can lead to profound insights and revelations about ourselves and our capabilities. By embracing uncertainty, we can push ourselves to overcome challenges and obstacles that we never thought possible. This can lead to a sense of empowerment and self-confidence that can positively impact every aspect of our lives.

In addition to personal growth, embracing uncertainty can also lead to professional growth and development. In a fast-paced and rapidly changing world, uncertainty is a constant presence in the workplace. Whether it's navigating a new project or adapting to changes in the market, embracing uncertainty allows us to be more flexible and adaptable in our professional lives. This can lead to new opportunities for career advancement and success. By viewing uncertainty as a chance to learn and grow, we can hone our problem-solving skills and develop a mindset that is conducive to innovation and creativity.

Furthermore, embracing uncertainty can also lead to emotional growth and resilience. When we face uncertainty with an open mind and a positive attitude, we are better able to cope with the stress and anxiety that it can bring. Instead of letting fear and doubt paralyze us, we can learn to be more resilient in the face of uncertainty. This can lead to a greater sense of emotional well-being and a more positive outlook on life. By embracing uncertainty as an opportunity for growth, we can cultivate a mindset of resilience and optimism that can help us navigate life's challenges with grace and poise.

One of the key principles of embracing uncertainty is the idea of letting go of the need for control. In a world that is constantly changing and evolving, it is impossible to predict or control every outcome. By letting go of the need for certainty and control, we can embrace uncertainty as a natural and necessary part of life. This requires a shift in mindset from one of fear and resistance to one of acceptance and openness. When we let go of the need for control, we can approach uncertainty with a sense of curiosity and wonder, rather than with fear and anxiety. This can lead to a more profound and enriching experience of life, as we learn to embrace the unknown with a sense of excitement and possibility.

Another important aspect of embracing uncertainty is the idea of reframing challenges as opportunities. When we face uncertain situations, it can be easy to view them as obstacles or barriers to our success. However, by reframing uncertainty as an opportunity for growth, we can see challenges in a new light. Instead of seeing uncertainty as something to be feared or avoided, we can view it as a chance to learn and grow. This can shift our perspective from one of limitation to one of possibility, opening up new avenues for personal and professional development. By reframing uncertainty as an opportunity for growth, we can approach life with a sense of optimism and enthusiasm, rather than with trepidation and apprehension. By viewing uncertainty as a chance to learn and grow, we can open ourselves up to new opportunities and experiences that can enrich our lives in countless ways. By letting go of the need for control and reframing challenges as opportunities, we can cultivate a mindset of resilience and optimism that can help us navigate life's uncertainties with grace and poise. Embracing uncertainty is not always easy, but the rewards of personal growth, emotional resilience, and professional development make it well worth the effort. So, the next time you find yourself facing the unknown, remember to embrace uncertainty as an opportunity for growth and watch as your life transforms in ways you never thought possible.

- Building Resilience in the Face of Challenges

Resilience is a key trait that allows individuals to bounce back from tough situations and challenges. In today's fast-paced and ever-changing world, it is essential to develop this quality in order to navigate the obstacles that come our way. Building resilience involves adopting a positive mindset, developing coping strategies, and cultivating a support system that can help us through difficult times. By actively working on building resilience, individuals can not only overcome challenges but also grow stronger and more adaptable in the face of adversity.

One of the first steps in building resilience is recognizing and accepting that challenges are a part of life. It is important to understand that no one is immune to facing difficulties, and that setbacks are an inevitable part of the human experience. By acknowledging this reality, individuals can begin to shift their perspective and view challenges as opportunities for growth and learning. This shift in mindset is crucial in building resilience, as it allows individuals to approach challenges with a sense of optimism and determination, rather than fear and defeat.

In addition to adopting a positive mindset, developing coping strategies is another key aspect of building resilience. Coping strategies are tools and techniques that individuals can use to manage stress, regulate emotions, and navigate difficult situations. These strategies can include relaxation techniques such as deep breathing or meditation, seeking social support from friends or family, engaging in physical activity, or practicing mindfulness and self-care. By developing a toolbox of coping strategies, individuals can build their resilience and better equip themselves to handle the challenges that come their way.

Furthermore, cultivating a support system is essential in building resilience. Having a strong support system can provide individuals with the emotional, practical, and social support they need to navigate tough times. This support system may include friends, family, colleagues, mentors, or mental health professionals who can offer encouragement, guidance, and a listening ear. By surrounding themselves with caring and supportive individuals, individuals can build their resilience and feel more empowered to face challenges head-on.

Building resilience is a lifelong process that requires commitment, self-awareness, and practice. It is important for individuals to consistently work on strengthening their resilience skills in order to effectively cope with the ups and downs of life. By cultivating a positive mindset, developing coping strategies, and building a strong support system, individuals can enhance their resilience and become better equipped to face challenges with courage and resilience. In doing so, they can not only overcome obstacles but also grow and thrive in the face of adversity.

Chapter 18: Conclusion

- REFLECTING ON YOUR Success Blueprint Journey

Reflecting on your Success Blueprint journey can be a deeply rewarding and enlightening experience. It is a time to pause and evaluate the progress you have made towards achieving your goals and ambitions. The success blueprint is essentially a roadmap that guides you towards your desired destination - whether that be personal or professional success, financial independence, or a fulfilling career. By reflecting on this journey, you can gain valuable insights into what has worked well for you, what obstacles you have overcome, and what areas you may need to refocus on moving forward.

One of the key benefits of reflecting on your success blueprint journey is gaining a better understanding of your strengths and weaknesses. By looking back on the goals you have achieved and the challenges you have faced, you can identify patterns in your behavior and decision-making process. This self-awareness can be crucial in helping you make more informed choices in the future and play to your strengths. It can also highlight areas where you may need to seek further development or support in order to continue making progress towards your goals.

Additionally, reflecting on your success blueprint journey can provide a sense of accomplishment and motivation. Celebrating the milestones and achievements along the way can boost your confidence and self-belief, helping you to stay motivated and focused on your long-term goals. It can also be a reminder of the hard work and dedication that has gone into reaching this point, reinforcing your commitment to continue pushing forward towards success. This sense of accomplishment can fuel your drive to overcome future challenges and setbacks, knowing that you have the resilience and determination to persevere.

Furthermore, reflecting on your success blueprint journey can help you identify areas for growth and improvement. It is an opportunity to assess the strategies and tactics you have employed thus far and determine what has been effective and what may need to be adjusted. By critically evaluating your progress, you can refine your approach and make strategic changes to better align with your goals and objectives. This reflective process can also spark new ideas and insights, inspiring you to think creatively and innovate in order to continue advancing towards your ultimate vision of success. By examining your strengths and weaknesses, celebrating your accomplishments, and identifying areas for growth, you can gain a deeper understanding of your journey and make informed decisions moving forward. This reflective process can bolster your confidence, motivation, and resilience, equipping you with the tools and mindset needed to overcome challenges and continue on the path towards success. So take the time to pause, reflect, and celebrate how far you have come - and use that insight to propel yourself even further towards your ultimate goals.

- Celebrating Your Achievements

Achieving success and reaching important milestones in life is an incredible accomplishment that deserves recognition and celebration. Whether it's landing a new job, completing a degree, starting a business, or achieving a personal goal, taking the time to acknowledge and celebrate your achievements is essential for your overall well-being and motivation. By recognizing your efforts and hard work, you not only boost your self-esteem and confidence but also inspire others around you to pursue their own goals and dreams.

Celebrating your achievements can take many forms, from throwing a party with friends and family to treating yourself to a special gift or experience. It's important to commemorate your successes in a way that feels meaningful and enjoyable to you, whether it's a small gesture or a larger event. Recognizing your accomplishments allows you to reflect on how far you've come and the challenges you've overcome, reminding yourself of your strengths and capabilities. This can help you stay motivated and focused on achieving even more in the future.

In addition to personal celebrations, it's also important to share your successes with others and acknowledge the contributions of those who have supported and helped you along the way. Whether it's thanking a mentor, colleague, friend, or family member for their guidance and encouragement, recognizing the role that others play in your achievements is a key part of celebrating your successes. By expressing gratitude and appreciation to those who have helped you succeed, you not only strengthen your relationships but also create a sense of community and shared accomplishment.

Furthermore, celebrating your achievements can also have a positive impact on your mental and emotional well-being. Taking the time to acknowledge and celebrate your successes can boost your mood, reduce stress, and increase your overall sense of happiness and fulfillment. By focusing on the positive aspects of your life and recognizing your accomplishments, you can build resilience and a positive outlook that can help you navigate future challenges and setbacks with confidence and optimism.

It's important to remember that celebrating your achievements is not about bragging or seeking validation from others. Instead, it's about recognizing your own worth and giving yourself the credit and praise you deserve for your hard work and dedication. By celebrating your successes, you show yourself and others that you value your accomplishments and are proud of the progress you've made. This can help build your self-confidence and self-esteem, making you more resilient and better equipped to face future challenges and pursue new goals and aspirations. Whether it's a small gesture or a larger event, taking the time to recognize and celebrate your successes is an important part of maintaining your motivation and well-being. By sharing your successes with others, expressing gratitude, and focusing on the positive aspects of your life, you can create a sense of accomplishment and fulfillment that will drive you to even greater success in the future. So go ahead, toast to your achievements and celebrate all that you've accomplished – you've earned it.

- Looking Ahead to Future Growth and Development

Looking ahead to future growth and development, it is crucial for organizations to strategically plan and prepare for the challenges and opportunities that lie ahead. In today's rapidly changing and increasingly competitive business environment, adaptability and foresight are key to staying ahead of the curve. By anticipating trends, identifying emerging markets, and leveraging technological advancements, businesses can position themselves for sustainable growth and success in the long term.

One of the key factors to consider when looking ahead to future growth and development is the evolving consumer landscape. With advances in technology and the rise of e-commerce, consumer behaviors and preferences are constantly shifting. Understanding these changes and adapting strategies to meet the needs of today's discerning customers is essential for businesses to thrive. This may involve investing in digital marketing, enhancing customer engagement through personalized experiences, and developing innovative products and services that resonate with target audiences.

Furthermore, organizations must also be mindful of the impact of globalization on their growth and development strategies. As borders blur and markets become increasingly interconnected, businesses have access to a broader customer base and a wealth of opportunities for expansion. However, this also means facing more competition and navigating complex regulatory environments. By staying informed about global trends, exploring new markets, and building strategic partnerships, companies can capitalize on the benefits of globalization while mitigating potential risks.

In addition to external factors, internal capabilities and resources play a crucial role in driving growth and development for organizations. Building a strong organizational culture that fosters innovation, collaboration, and continuous learning is essential for staying competitive in today's dynamic business landscape. Investing in talent development, leadership training, and employee engagement initiatives can help organizations attract and retain top talent, foster creativity and productivity, and drive long-term success.

Another important aspect to consider when looking ahead to future growth and development is the role of technology in shaping business strategies. With advancements in artificial intelligence, data analytics, and automation, businesses have access to powerful tools that can streamline processes, enhance decision-making, and drive efficiency. By embracing digital transformation and integrating technology into all aspects of operations, organizations can position themselves for sustainable growth and competitive advantage in the digital age.

Moreover, sustainability and corporate social responsibility are becoming increasingly important considerations for businesses looking to achieve long-term growth and development. Consumers are placing greater emphasis on ethical practices, environmental stewardship, and social impact when making purchasing decisions. By incorporating sustainability into their business strategies, organizations can not only enhance their brand reputation and customer loyalty but also contribute to the greater good of society and the planet. By anticipating trends, understanding consumer behaviors, leveraging technology, and embracing sustainability, organizations can position themselves for sustainable growth and success in the long term. Through continuous innovation, adaptability, and a commitment to excellence, businesses can overcome challenges, seize opportunities, and drive meaningful impact in an ever-changing world.